Encounters with
Jesus

Encounters with
Jesus

When Ordinary People Met the Savior

Richard D. Phillips

P&R
P U B L I S H I N G
P.O. BOX 817 • PHILLIPSBURG • NEW JERSEY 08865-0817

Page design by Tobias Design
Typesetting by Michelle Feaster

Printed in the United States of America

Library of Congress Cataloging-in-Publication Data

Phillips, Richard D. (Richard David), 1960–
    Encounters with Jesus : ordinary people who met the Savior / Richard D. Phillips.
        p.   cm.
    Includes bibliographical references and index.
    ISBN 0-87552-193-2 (pbk.)
    1. Jesus Christ—Biography. 2. Bible. N.T.—Biography. I. Title.

BT301.2 .P475 2002
232.9'5—dc21

                                                    2001052309

To

HANNAH CATHERINE PHILLIPS,
with all my heart

(John 17:3)

and to

THE SON OF MAN,
who came not to be served but to serve,
and to give his life as a ransom for many

(Matt. 20:28)

Contents

Preface

Some of the most interesting and exciting portions of the Bible are those that show Jesus Christ in his dealings with individual men and women. The thirteen encounters between Jesus and ordinary people this book presents are that and more. They are windows into what it was like to see and speak with Jesus during the days he walked upon this earth. They also are of the greatest value for instructing our faith, since they contain spiritual truths that Jesus pressed upon those with whom he interacted. The apostle Peter wrote, "Though you have not seen him, you love him" (1 Peter 1:8), and for that reason Christians are bound to love these accounts because of the intimacy with which they approach our Savior. Furthermore, the matters he chose to emphasize in these encounters are not ones we can afford to ignore. It was to the men and women of these Gospel accounts that Jesus spoke in those bygone days, but it was for us that the Holy Spirit inspired their accounts in Scripture.

It was for these reasons, to see and to show Jesus Christ, that I first was interested in preaching and then writing about these encounters. Both I and others have found these studies helpful on a number of dimensions. First, to watch Jesus in his dealings with others is to gain great insight for our relationship with him. The way he treated others speaks of how he will treat us, whether to teach or reprove or encourage. Second, these accounts of Christ's ministry aid us in ministry to others within the family of believers, as we counsel and comfort, reprove and exhort one another in the church. Finally, these studies shed a bright light on how we are to live before an unbelieving world, on how Christ encountered unbelief, and therefore how we ought to go about the task of evangelism he has given to us. I pray that in all of these ways, these encounters with Jesus will prove profitable to you. But more than that, I pray that you will come seeking to see and to hear and to encounter him for yourself, whom to know is life eternal.

In acknowledging my debt to others, I first want to thank my wife, Sharon, and our children, who so wonderfully support my active ministry of preaching, pastoring, and writing. Sharon wrote the discussion questions, and I am grateful for her help in making the book more useful for small-group studies. This book is dedicated to my daughter Hannah, with prayers that as she grows up in the church she will not merely know about Jesus, her parents' Savior and Friend, but also know him for herself and thereby have eternal life.

I am grateful to my partner in preaching, Dr. Philip G. Ryken, for so much meaningful fellowship and valuable advice, and to my assistant, Patricia Russell, for her invaluable help in the whole of my ministry. I am again indebted to my friends Lee Beckham, Bruce Bell, and Jen Brewer for their kindness in reading these chapters and making many helpful suggestions that have improved the book significantly.

These messages were preached in the summer and fall of 2000 to the congregation of Tenth Presbyterian Church in Philadelphia during the weeks of our strong grief over the death of our long-time pastor, James Montgomery Boice. These studies on the person of our wonderful Lord were a source of much comfort to me and, I believe, many others. I am grateful to God for the special presence of his Spirit during our time of need, and to many Christians for their loving prayers.

Finally, I give my heartfelt thanks to the session and congregation of Tenth Presbyterian Church, for the opportunity to spend so much time in study of God's Word and for so great a multitude of prayers and love.

Jesus and the Scholar

John 3:1–21

Now there was a man of the Pharisees named Nicodemus, a member of the Jewish ruling council. He came to Jesus at night and said, "Rabbi, we know you are a teacher who has come from God." (John 3:1–2)

It was Jesus' first visit to Jerusalem after the beginning of his earthly ministry. John's account of it is brief. Jesus went up for the Passover, arriving in the temple to find the money-changers and sellers of cattle, sheep, and doves there. Making a whip out of cords, he drove all these out, crying, "How dare you turn my Father's house into a market!" (John 2:16). This led to what seems to have been Jesus' first confrontation with the religious leaders. John concludes the account of this visit by saying, "While he was in Jerusalem at the Passover Feast, many people saw the miraculous signs he was doing and believed in his name. But Jesus would not entrust himself to them, for he knew all men. He did not need man's testimony about man, for he knew what was in a man" (John 2:23–25).

That is the background in which the encounter takes place between Jesus and the scholar, Nicodemus. This passage begins with the words "Now there was a man of the Pharisees named Nicodemus." It is immediately obvious that John intends to use this man as an example of what he was writing about in John 2, the kind of man who saw Jesus and had a certain belief in him. It would have been easier for John to write, "Now there was a Pharisee. . . ." Instead he wrote, "Now there was a man of the Pharisees." The connection is clear: "Jesus knew what was in a man. . . . Now there was a man." Nicodemus came to Jesus, therefore, as the representative of those who possess a certain belief in Jesus, a certain regard for him, but one that Jesus neither accepts nor embraces.

Nicodemus the Scholar

Marginal believers could hardly have a better representative than Nicodemus. We can readily discern three things about him, beginning with his identity as a Pharisee.

People today do not think highly of Pharisees because of the things Jesus exposed about them during his ministry, particularly their self-righteous hypocrisy. However true that may be, it is also true that they were the most respected people of their time. Jesus' problems with the Pharisees stemmed from their religious practice and teaching. But one thing that could not be denied was that they were exceedingly moral. They dedicated their lives not only to reading the law and preserving it, as did the scribes, but also to keeping its commandments and regulations. The Pharisees were a sect of men, never numerous, who lived above the common level of life and enjoyed the great respect of everyone around them. Such a man was Nicodemus, an exemplar of moral conduct.

The second thing we learn about Nicodemus is that he was a leader of the people. He was "a member of the Jewish ruling council" (John 3:1). This would be the Sanhedrin, the highest ruling body among the Jews in that day. Therefore Nicodemus was a member of the ruling elite.

Third, we can be sure that Nicodemus was a scholar. All Pharisees were devoted students of Scripture. It is noteworthy, however, that Nicodemus is a Greek name. Upperclass Jews often gave their children Jewish and Greek names, signifying the two worlds in which they traveled. Having adopted his Greek name, Nicodemus must have been a student and admirer of the philosophers. Also the name Nicodemus appears in the records of high officials as early as 68 B.C. and as late as A.D. 70, so it is possible that he belonged to a powerful and distinguished family.

Nicodemus was not merely a man, but he was quite a man. It is hard to pick a similar figure from our era who so combines political power with ethical excellence and erudite scholarship. If man were to have a representative in Jerusalem, if those who saw and possessed a belief in Jesus could have but one delegate, there could hardly be one more fitting than Nicodemus. It is nothing short of amazing that a man of his stature should come to see a carpenter turned prophet. Yet that is what he did.

That is Nicodemus. Why, then, did he come? This is the first in a series of studies on encounters with Jesus in the

Gospels. One thing we want to do in each case is ask what brought the person to Jesus or Jesus to the person. In this case it is evident. Nicodemus had observed Jesus and had seen the miraculous signs spoken of in John 2:23. These intrigued him and led him to seek an audience with this wonder worker, albeit a discreet and secret meeting, as our passage shows. John 3:2 tells of his coming to Jesus. "He came to Jesus at night and said, 'Rabbi, we know you are a teacher who has come from God. For no one could perform the miraculous signs you are doing if God were not with him.'"

The first thing we notice is that Nicodemus came under cover of darkness. Evidently he did not wish to be discovered coming to Jesus, did not want to compromise himself with his fellow Pharisees and power brokers. He had seen Jesus, he was obviously impressed, and yet he was not prepared to commit himself to this upstart from Galilee.

"Rabbi," he said, showing respect, "we know that you are a teacher who has come from God." There is, I believe, more than a hint of patronage in those words. "We know," he says, making Jesus aware that he speaks for powerful others who have condescended to give him a favorable report. Nicodemus comes as one with strength of position and resources. He acts as the one with the initiative, with something to offer. This may have been a simple inquiry, an initial and tentative contact. But I don't think it is too much to say that he meant to impress upon Jesus the authority of his position, even to co-opt Jesus at this early stage of his ministry. He might have gone on to remark, "We know you are from God. But we have been serving God here in Jerusalem for some time. Things are much different here than way out in Nazareth. You are going to need good advice, handling, support, and resources. You would be well advised to let us guide you in your affairs."

I don't know for sure that Nicodemus was going to say these things, because Jesus cut him off long before he could. We see what he did say, and that tells us quite a lot. The key phrase was "we know." Nicodemus comes bearing his judgment, the appraisal of his party, the wisdom and insight of scholars and leaders.

What Nicodemus knows is that Jesus is "a teacher who has come from God." He knows that he is a teacher—that is all. Nicodemus reminds us of the many people today and in every age who are eager to compliment Jesus so long as he remains just a teacher. The learned scholars condescend to approve of him; the leaders of thought and fashion give their considered praise. How different this is from those commended in Scripture for true faith, those who rush to him crying, "Savior, have mercy on us!" Or as the apostle Thomas would realize at the end of this Gospel, falling before Jesus and worshiping, "My Lord and my God!" (John 20:28). I have no doubt that Nicodemus came to Jesus with good will, but it was that of an equal, that of a patron, and not that of a believer in his Savior, a worshiper before his God.

"You Must Be Born Again"

It is significant that Jesus did not welcome this advance, did not give one bit of encouragement to Nicodemus. Had Jesus been a mere teacher, a mere man, even one God was with, these words would have been music to his ears. He is recognized, accorded access, promised support. Any mere man would have been delighted at such news. But Jesus bluntly replies that Nicodemus does not know what he is talking about. He is not in a position to know. "I tell you the truth," Jesus said, "no one can see the kingdom of God unless he is born again" (John 3:3).

That was Jesus' reply, and we can be sure that it was a reproof, but a reproof targeted to push Nicodemus in the direction of real faith. A comparison with other encounters will help us to see what Jesus was doing. When speaking to the rich young ruler, so devoted to his money, Jesus commanded, "Sell all you have and give it to the poor." To the crowd grateful for the miraculous food he provided, he replied, "Labor not for food that perishes." To the woman at the well, come to draw her water, Jesus offered "living water." And to the confident Pharisee, proud of his lineage, he replied, "You must be born again." Leon Morris writes, "In one sentence He sweeps away all that Nicodemus stood for, and demands that he be remade by the power of God."[1]

But it is not only Nicodemus who needs to be born again; as Jesus proclaims, "No one can see the kingdom of God unless he is born again." This is one of the great statements of the Bible. Jesus proclaims that salvation requires not a mere superficial change, not just moral reformation, not just the grasping of ideas. J. C. Ryle says, "It is a thorough change of heart, will, and character. It is a resurrection. It is a new creation. It is a passing from death to life. It is the implanting in our dead hearts a new principle from above."[2]

The expression "born again" can also be translated as "born from above." The Greek word is *anōthen*, which combines the adverb *above* with the suffix *from*. It is found five other times in the New Testament, including in John 3:31, and in each of those occasions it is translated as "from above."

In that case, Jesus is saying, "You must be born from

above." That is the point John's Gospel makes in its prologue, where the apostle writes, "To all who received him, to those who believed in his name, he gave the right to become children of God—children born not of natural descent, nor of human decision or a husband's will, but born of God" (John 1:12–13). The new birth Jesus is talking about is one that is from above, that is, of God.

Nonetheless Nicodemus's response reveals that he took Jesus' meaning to be born "again," so we must not reject that translation. "Surely," he asked, a man "cannot enter a second time into his mother's womb to be born!" (John 3:4). This is one of many occasions when the apostle John intentionally uses a word that conveys a double meaning: born again, born from above.

Jesus answered Nicodemus's question by giving another description of what he was talking about: "I tell you the truth, no one can enter the kingdom of God unless he is born of water and the Spirit" (John 3:5).

When it comes to the meaning of "water and spirit," there are about as many interpretations as there are commentators. There are, however, three main views. The first is that water symbolizes baptism and the spirit refers to conversion as the work of the Holy Spirit. Generally speaking, those who have a high view of baptism tend to opt for this interpretation, including Roman Catholics, Lutherans, and many Reformed scholars. The obvious problem with this view is that nothing in this context connects water with baptism. Furthermore, it is hard to see how Nicodemus would be expected to make the connection with a sacrament that had not yet been instituted. John the Baptist's activity, noted earlier in John's Gospel (1:15–34), makes this connection possible if still improbable.

The second view is that water and spirit each refer to

two different births, one natural (from a mother's womb) and the other supernatural. Natural childbirth involves the breaking of water, and the point would be that you have to be born once of water and again by the Spirit. This idea of two births seems to go along with John 3:6, which says, "Flesh gives birth to flesh, but the Spirit gives birth to spirit."

The third view, and I think the best, begins by observing that in the original text the grammatical structure of "water and spirit" favors a single description of the new birth rather two different births.[3] It also assumes, I think reasonably, that if Jesus chides Nicodemus as a teacher of Israel for not understanding "these things," as he does in John 3:10, then this must be something taught in the Old Testament. If you look there for "water and spirit" you will find it, and you find it in one of the key passages that talks about the subject Jesus has in mind, spiritual regeneration. The passage is Ezekiel 36:25–27:

> I will sprinkle clean water on you, and you will be clean; I will cleanse you from all your impurities and from all your idols. I will give you a new heart and put a new spirit in you; I will remove from you your heart of stone and give you a heart of flesh. And I will put my Spirit in you and move you to follow my decrees and be careful to keep my laws.

This is a rebirth from above, and one a teacher like Nicodemus should be familiar with. Here, new birth, birth from above, means cleansing from sin as by water and the transformation of the heart by the Spirit of God so that those who once were rebels against God are now made his willing followers. That is what the new birth is all about.

Jesus' Teaching on the New Birth

Let me summarize what Jesus says in this passage about the new birth. First, *the new birth is necessary* for you to enter, or even to see, the kingdom of God. By this, Jesus means salvation and eternal life. Unless you are made a new person, you cannot be saved. You, like Nicodemus, might see the man Jesus, but you do not see the kingdom of God, you do not believe unto salvation. The reason for this is that apart from God's regenerating work, you are neither willing to be saved nor interested in salvation. As Jesus says, "Flesh gives birth to flesh, but the Spirit gives birth to spirit" (John 3:6). Martyn Lloyd-Jones explains:

> Whereas those who are not Christians are not interested in spiritual things, the Christian is. The world is not interested in the affairs of the soul at all and tries to avoid considering them. The world is spiritually dead, dead in trespasses and sins and it regards spiritual things as utterly boring. It wants to enjoy the world, it is out for the glittering prizes that the world has to offer. But the Christian has been made spiritually alive. He is very concerned about the affairs of the soul, they are the things that come first in his life and in all his thinking. How then has this happened? It is the power of Christ that has come upon him: "God has made us alive with Christ even when we were dead in transgressions" (Eph. 2:5).[4]

Not only must you be born again to enter the kingdom of God, as John 3:5 says, but also the new birth is necessary even to see it (John 3:3). Nicodemus began by talking about all that he knew. But without a rebirth by the Holy Spirit, there is no knowledge of spiritual things. He could be vastly learned, and learning is a good thing. He could investigate the records and hold seminars and write papers, but unless God should bring about a new birth, a new heart, and a new light in the mind, the natural man does not receive the things that come from God.

I was reminded of this recently by a television special called *The Search for Jesus*. The journalist in charge of this project stated that they wanted to do an objective investigation. To achieve this they began by taking a skeptical view of the Bible and looking for the facts. That, of course, is not objective. It was no surprise to me to learn that they could not arrive at any claim higher for Jesus than that of Nicodemus: He was a teacher.[5] Whenever you begin by boasting about what you know or can know apart from God's revelation, then, as with Nicodemus, flesh begets only flesh while remaining blind to the things that come only by the Spirit.

The problem is not that we lack evidence for Jesus but that we are unwilling to humble ourselves as condemned sinners and admit that we need a Savior. Nicodemus saw Jesus performing his miracles in Jerusalem, and by the flesh alone he could not receive eternal life by faith. As Paul writes in 1 Corinthians 2:14, "The man without the Spirit does not accept the things that come from the Spirit of God, for they are foolishness to him, and he cannot understand them, because they are spiritually discerned." This is also a reminder to Christians, and especially to Christian scholars and preachers, that without the illuminating work of God's Spirit our labor too is all in vain.

The second point that is clear in Jesus' teaching is that *the new birth is God's work and not man's.* This is seen in the terminology "born from above." Just as we do not bring about our natural birth, so also our spiritual rebirth is not our work. It is the work of another, even the work of God. It is the work of his grace. Morris observes, "Entry into the kingdom is not by way of human striving, but by that rebirth which only God can effect."[6]

Third, Jesus points out that while the working of the new birth is invisible—it is impossible for us to see it happening or even to understand its mechanism—nonetheless *it is revealed by its effects*. That is the point of John 3:8, "The wind blows wherever it pleases. You hear its sound, but you cannot tell where it comes from or where it is going. So it is with everyone born of the Spirit."

That was also the point in Ezekiel 36, which Jesus, I think, has in mind: "I will cleanse you from all your impurities and from all your idols. . . . I will put my Spirit in you and move you to follow my decrees and be careful to keep my laws" (vv. 25, 27). The new birth has a purpose, and it is recognized by its visible effects. The next chapter of Ezekiel contains the great passage about the valley of dry bones, where the breath or Spirit of God comes and brings life. "This is what the Sovereign LORD says: 'Come from the four winds, O breath, and breathe into these slain, that they may live' " (Ezek. 37:9). That well matches what Jesus is talking about in John 3:8. In both cases, the "blowing" of the Holy Spirit causes spiritually dead people to show signs of life. The point is that new life is the evidence of the new birth. If there are no signs of new and different life, then there is no reason to think there has been a rebirth.

The term "born again" has entered into our common speech and therefore has become greatly abused. People have an intense emotional experience and thereafter claim to be born again. But unless you have come to look on Jesus Christ as your Savior from sin and then have entered into a new life, one characterized by a growing relationship with him and increasing obedience to God, then what Jesus is talking about here has not happened to you. The new birth is revealed by its effects.

The most important point is that if you have not been born again by the sovereign grace of God, you not only cannot enter the kingdom of God, as Jesus says in John 3:5, but also you cannot see it when it is before your eyes. You, like Nicodemus and so many unbelieving scholars in our time, cannot recognize Jesus for what he is when he is before you. What you need is not more human investigation, not scholarly debate, but humble repentance and grace to cry to God for mercy.

How Can This Be?

This leads to Nicodemus's final question, "How can this be?" (John 3:9). Jesus began by reproving this great leader and teacher for failing to understand the simple things of God's Word. But then, no doubt out of his compassion for the man who came to see him, Jesus went on to answer that question most thoroughly.

Jesus gives three answers in John 3:14–21, beginning with *the means of rebirth*. "How can the new birth be?" Nicodemus asks. Jesus replies, "Just as Moses lifted up the snake in the desert, so the Son of Man must be lifted up, that everyone who believes in him may have eternal life" (vv. 14–15). Jesus is recalling an event from the time of Moses, recorded in Numbers 21. The Israelites were beset by fiery serpents, and God had Moses make a snake of bronze and set it on a pole. Those who looked upon the bronze snake were healed. This is how Jesus answers the question How can the new birth be? The answer is that God has lifted up the Son of Man, that is, the Savior of men from heaven, so that everyone who looks to him in faith shall be saved, shall "have eternal life."

The issue is not how you can procure a new birth but how God grants it to sinners. The answer is found at the cross of Jesus Christ, where he was lifted up. Christ's sacrificial death was God's plan for the rebirth of sinners. There are two "musts" in this passage. Jesus says, "You must be born again." But then he teaches, "The Son of Man must be lifted up." Those two "musts" go together: Christ crucified, bearing our sins, and the regeneration of those who were lost but now look to him in faith. That is how the new birth takes place: Christ dying for sinners who receive grace to believe from the Spirit. Christ lifted up is God's provision for those dead in sin who must be born again; the cross is the means by which Jesus secures the Spirit for the regeneration of our hearts.

Jesus' second answer comes in John 3:16–17, where he deals with *the source of the new birth*. "How can this be?" the scholar asked. Jesus replies with these great words, "For God so loved the world that he gave his one and only Son, that whoever believes in him shall not perish but have eternal life." The reason there is a new birth is that God loved the world. The world was in rebellion against him. All mankind together was in league to deny his glory, to reject his authority, to despise his will. The evidence of this was all around in Jesus' day, and it is all around us today. But God so loved the world—that is why there is a rebirth.

How different is God's love from ours. We love when there is something lovable, something lovely to us. But God loves the unloved and the unlovely. God loves this world. People are always saying, "Why doesn't God do something?" But he has! He has given the new birth, the new creation, the resurrection life through Jesus Christ.

I hope you see what this means. It means that there is hope for this world and for you. You can have a new start. Why? Because God so loved. You can have a new life. How? By receiving God's gift through faith in his Son. You can have a new beginning, be a new man, a new woman. Is there any message more glorious, more wonderful, more important than that? How can this be? Because God so loved the world that he gave his only Son, "that whoever believes in him shall not perish but have eternal life."

The third answer is found beginning in John 3:19: "Light has come into the world." "How can this rebirth be?" Because Jesus has come as a light shining into the darkness, and those who look to him are enabled to see. John's prologue said of him, "In him was life, and that life was the light of men. . . . The true light that gives light to every man was coming into the world" (John 1:4, 9). Man in sin could not see the kingdom of God, could not enter into eternal life. So Jesus came as the light by which we can see, as the way to the kingdom of God.

What an answer that is to Nicodemus's question! G. Campbell Morgan sums it up so well:

> "How?" he asked. Jesus replied, "Life through my death; love from the heart of God through His gift; light through My mission in the world. That is How. Because God so loved, He gave; and life comes through that gift, and now the light is shining."[7]

The Light Is Shining

There was one last point for Jesus to make, namely, his challenge to the scholar who came by night. "This is the verdict," he said. "Light has come into the world, but men loved darkness instead of light because their deeds were evil. . . . But whoever lives by the truth comes into the light" (John 3:19, 21).

You see the point. Once the light had come, it was Nicodemus and not Jesus who was under scrutiny. To reject the light is self-condemnation, and now the light is shining (John 3:18). The coming of the light created a crisis for the scholar; indeed, that is the Greek word that translates as "verdict"—*krisis*. The scholar could commit himself to Jesus, believe on him not merely as teacher but as Savior of his soul. Or he could stand condemned because he had seen the light but turned away to darkness. That is the same crisis that faces each and every one today who hears the gospel, including you—a crisis that results in either condemnation through unbelief or salvation and eternal life through belief in the Son of God.

Nicodemus shows up again in John's Gospel. In John 7 we are told that he spoke up for Jesus before the Sanhedrin. But still he stood outside the circle of Jesus' light, and yet the light was still shining. The day finally came when the Son of Man was lifted up, and Nicodemus was there. Surely he recalled this conversation as he stood and gazed upon Jesus dying on the cross. "The Son of Man must be lifted up, that everyone who believes in him may have eternal life" (John 3:14–15). Finally, then, the scholar saw the kingdom of God. He saw not merely a teacher, not simply a rabbi, not just a worker of wonders. He saw upon that cross the Savior of his soul; he saw his redemption by the shedding of Christ's precious blood.

That is when Nicodemus at long last came out of the darkness and into the light. We read in John 19:38–39, "Joseph of Arimathea asked Pilate for the body of Jesus. Now Joseph was a disciple of Jesus, but secretly because he feared the Jews. With Pilate's permission, he came and took the body away. He was accompanied by Nicodemus, the man who earlier had visited Jesus at night." Finally Nicodemus committed himself to Jesus, was willing to be known as his disciple, come what may. "So it is," Jesus had said to him, "with everyone born of the Spirit."

The light is still shining through the preaching of this gospel. Do not wait, like Nicodemus did, but look now upon the Son of Man lifted up, and you will see there the love of God for you. And if you see your Savior, it is because his light has shown you the kingdom of God so that you too are born again, born from above, into everlasting life.

Jesus and the Woman at the Well

John 4:1–30

The woman said, "I know that Messiah" (called Christ) "is coming. When he comes, he will explain everything to us." Then Jesus declared, "I who speak to you am he."
(John 4:25–26)

It is said that truth is stranger than fiction. When it comes to the Bible, and especially to the life of Jesus Christ, I would like to amend that saying to read, "Truth is more marvelous than fiction." In support of that proposal I present this encounter between Jesus and the woman at the well in John 4. There is no more powerful or beautiful story than the true account of this wonderful meeting.

Consider the characters. First, there is a woman, at a

time when women had practically no status or power. Second, she is a Samaritan, that is, a member of a marginalized and outcast race. Third, everything about this woman speaks of scandal and disgrace. She is at the well fetching her water at a time when the other village women have cleared out. She is suspicious in her attitude but also open to glimmers of hope.

Consider next the man who comes up to the well where she gets her water. In appearance he is everything that is a threat to her. He is a man, a teacher with disciples, and a Jew under the law. This was the most predictable of encounters; it could happen a thousand times with only one possible result. But this encounter bears the most unpredictable outcome. The Samaritan woman becomes a disciple of the Jewish rabbi and shares his gospel all around. The woman in disgrace is made an agent of grace. In the center is Jesus, who with total control reveals himself not merely as a man of the Jews but as a Savior for the world.

To Seek and to Save

In our studies of these encounters with Jesus, we want to ask what brought each of the parties together, in this case the woman and our Lord. John tells us it was about the sixth hour, that is, around noon, and she came alone to draw her water. Later we find that she is a woman of scandal, she lives with a man to whom she is not married, and she has had five husbands beforehand. It is natural to conclude, therefore, that these facts are related—the reason she is walking alone to the well a considerable distance in the heat of the day is because she is unwelcome with the other women at more attractive times. The most basic and repetitive tasks are always the most social ones—when we

think of village women sewing or washing clothes or fetching water, it is always in company. But the ancient Near
East, even in Samaria, was not a tolerant society, particularly toward the sexual sins of women. So it is no stretch to
imagine that she comes alone to the well at this time because she is unwelcome in wholesome society. She is a picture, in this respect, of sin's alienating power.

We ask why the woman was at the well, but the real
mystery is why Jesus was at the well. There are good reasons
why we might find this surprising. For one thing, Jesus was
at the well because he was thirsty. John writes, "Jesus, tired
as he was from the journey, sat down by the well" (John
4:6). The problem with this is the claim to Jesus' divinity
that is so central to John's Gospel. Jesus is the Son of God;
he was, John wrote, "with God in the beginning. Through
him all things were made; without him nothing was made
that has been made" (John 1:2–3). How, then, can the divine Son and Fountainhead be thirsty? The answer is this
clear testimony to his full humanity. Yes, he is the Son of
God. But he is true man as well, and therefore in his humanity he thirsts and grows tired. Jesus was at the well because he had come into the world in true flesh, that he
might know us and help us in the weakness of our human
condition.

There is a second reason we are surprised to see Jesus
here, and that is because the well was in Samaria, a region
and a people despised by the Jews. Samaria was located directly between Judea in the south, where Jesus had been,
and Galilee in the north, where Jesus was going. Many, if
not most, Jews took the longer way around Samaria, by way
of the Jordan River, to avoid conflict with the Samaritans
and to show their disdain.

The animosity between Jews and Samaritans ran long

and deep. When the Assyrians conquered and annexed Israel's northern kingdom in 722 B.C., they brought in other peoples from all over. These Gentiles intermarried with the Israelites who remained, and eventually they tried to pick up Israel's old religion. In the sixth century B.C., the southern kingdom was also conquered, but after many years God graciously returned the Jews to their land intact. The books of Ezra and Nehemiah record this great return to the land, including their refusal to allow the half-breed Samaritans to have any part in the rebuilding of the temple in Jerusalem. The Samaritans built a temple on Mount Gerizim, near this well of Jacob's, and set up their rival religion. Tensions were high, especially when in the second century B.C. a Jewish king, John Hyrcanus, destroyed the Samaritan temple. Jews considered Samaritans unclean, and converse with Samaritan women was especially despised.

These dynamics are reflected in this account. Jesus was resting upon the well when the woman came up. He asked her for a drink of water, and she replied, "You are a Jew and I am a Samaritan woman. How can you ask me for a drink?" John adds for his readers, "For Jews do not associate with Samaritans" (John 4:9). Jews were not allowed to share utensils with Samaritans without becoming ceremonially unclean, a fact this woman knew. Her tone bristles with animosity. But Jesus' reply makes clear what he had in mind and what brought him to this well in Samaria: "If you knew the gift of God and who it is that asks you for a drink, you would have asked him and he would have given you living water" (John 4:10).

Here we have the answer of what brought Jesus to this encounter: his mission as the Savior of the world. What a contrast there is between Jesus and the Jews of his day—a contrast only begun by his willingness to sit and drink with this woman. The biggest contrast is that Jesus was eager for her salvation, while the Jews were indifferent or even intent upon the damnation of Samaritans and other Gentiles. The Jews resented the Samaritans' feeble attempts at their own religion and thereby spurned God's intention that they should be beacons of saving truth to the world. Here were the Samaritans on their doorstep, people who if half-Gentile were also half-Israelite, and the Jews made no effort at leading them out of the darkness and into the light of God's saving Word.

But where they would not go Jesus gladly went. Other Jews, though surely few, traveled down this road, if reluctantly. I suppose some Jews even sat upon this well. But they did not speak to Samaritan women. They did not humbly ask for a drink of water, and they did not speak of God's offer of grace. The Son of God came to this woman for the same reason he was born in Bethlehem in the weakness of an infant child: He came to be the Savior of the world, or as he put it, "The Son of Man came to seek and to save what was lost" (Luke 19:10).

If you find yourself encountering Jesus Christ, it is for the same reason. Whoever you are, whatever you have been, Jesus has come to you to become your Savior, to seek and to save you who have been lost.

Jesus' Evangelistic Example

Jesus sets an example of evangelism that is worthy of our attention. His encounter with this fallen woman began when he treated her with simple dignity. He did not treat her as a pariah but as a person. He started with a request, and that request opened the door to a relationship. The problem with so many Christians today is that we are walled off from the world the way the Jews of Jesus' time were. We do not travel through the world but only within the ghetto of our own subculture, and if we interact with the people of the world, we don't think they have anything to offer us. Small wonder, then, that they are not open to what we have to offer them. Jesus was not like that. He walked through the world and treated even scandalous Samaritan women as persons of worth, capable of giving him something of value. As Frederick Godet sagely notes, "He is not unaware that the way to gain a soul is often to ask a service of it."[1]

In passing we might observe the positive way Jesus treated women. Jesus is the greatest liberator of women, not by denying their womanhood or femininity but by doing what he did to this woman. Jesus is going to confront her sin with his grace and call her to his service for the extension of the gospel, and that is the greatest freedom there is.

The second thing Jesus did was to take the situation he was in and use it to point to spiritual realities. Jesus commonly did this. It was after feeding the crowd that he spoke of himself as the Bread of Life. And here by the well, he makes the analogy between the thirst of the body and the thirst of the soul.

Jesus began by saying, "If you knew the gift of God," and the point of evangelism is that people do not know it. It is this way today—people have no idea that God has something to give them, that God looks on them with care and with grace to save if only they will ask. Most people look upon God with the vague resentment this woman cast toward Jesus. He is a source of condemnation for what they do and who they are. They cannot escape the knowledge of God, nor therefore the conviction of sin. So God is an authority to be resisted, a judge to be resented. All the while they do not know the gift of God, which Jesus points out to this woman by means of a simple analogy.

Jesus speaks of "living water," which in their common speech meant running water. Living, or running, water is better than stagnant water, even water from a fine source like Jacob's well. This is how the woman took Jesus' words. "Where can you get this living water?" she asked. "Are you greater than our father Jacob, who gave us this well and drank from it himself?" (John 4:11–12). If the great patriarch Jacob had to dig a well to get water here, a well that had lasted all those centuries, who was this man to suggest he was able to provide running water instead? Like Nicodemus before her, this woman is unable to think above the worldly plane about what Jesus was saying. But Jesus pressed on with her, making one of the great statements of the Gospel of John: "Everyone who drinks this water will be thirsty again, but whoever drinks the water I give him will never thirst. Indeed, the water I give him will become in him a spring of water welling up to eternal life" (John 4:13–14).

Jesus contrasts the water Jacob's well provides with the spiritual fountain he offers unto eternal life. He says that man, even though he drinks the water of a well such as this, will still thirst, will have deep and unfilled longings. This is one of the great messages the Word of God brings into this world. The world is longing, its men and women thirst, and yet what the world has to offer is unable to satisfy that great thirst. Arthur Pink puts this in particularly stirring terms:

> Whether he articulates it or not the natural man, the world over, is crying "I thirst." Why this consuming desire to acquire wealth? Why this craving for the honors and plaudits of the world? Why this

mad rush after pleasure, the turning from one form of it to another with persistent and unwearied diligence? Why this eager search for wisdom—this scientific inquiry, this pursuit of philosophy, this ransacking of the writings of the ancients, and this ceaseless experimentation by the moderns? Why the insane craze for that which is novel? Why? Because there is an aching void in the soul. Because there is something remaining in every natural man that is *unsatisfied*. This is true of the millionaire equally as much as the pauper: the riches of the former bring no real contentment. It is as true of the globe-trotter equally as much as of the country rustic who has never been outside the bounds of his native country: travelling from one end of the earth to the other and back again fails to discover the secret of peace. Over all the cisterns of this world's providing is written in letters of ineffaceable truth, "Whosoever drinks of this water *shall thirst again*."[2]

The thirst of our soul is a spiritual thirst; therefore natural resources cannot quench it. It is, as Psalm 42 puts it, our soul that pants for God. We were made by God for God. We were made to worship him and to know him, and therefore he alone can fill the need of our soul. The gift that God gives, which Jesus speaks of here as living water, the world cannot give or take away.

The classic expression of this comes from the opening paragraph of Augustine's *Confessions*: "You have made us for yourself, and our heart is restless until it rests in you."[3] This is true not only for this Samaritan woman, but also it is true for you. You may have all this world can offer— riches, rank, place, and power—and yet be utterly unfulfilled. This more than anything else tells the story of our time. Amidst gaudy affluence and ready entertainment, with unparalleled leisure and earthly excitement, ours is a generation aching because of thirst, the thirst of the soul that only God can fill and that Jesus offers to us all. "Whoever drinks the water I give him will never thirst," he says. "Indeed, the water I give him will become in him a spring of water welling up to eternal life."

That is the Christian testimony, that in a world of death there is life for the taking. "I have come," Jesus said, "that they may have life, and have it to the full" (John 10:10). That is what Jesus offered and what we today offer in his name. Not a list of rules, not a political agenda, not a superficial association, but life welling up, even springing forth from within.

That is what eternal life is, a fountain with energy and force and joy and spiritual vitality working within the soul of all who have received from God the gift of salvation. One Puritan writer titled his book on Christian salvation "The life of God in the soul of man," and that is what Jesus is talking about, not a stagnant well but a springing fountain of life that no man can stop up. In this, Jesus was setting before this woman the fulfillment of what was promised in the Old Testament with so many similar expressions. This was the promise given through Isaiah:

> With joy you will draw water
> from the wells of salvation. (Isa. 12:3)

Perhaps the clearest expression comes from Psalm 36:

> They feast on the abundance of your house;
> you give them drink from your river of delights.

> For with you is the fountain of life;
>> in your light we see light. (vv. 8–9)

Therefore, as James Montgomery Boice says in one of the hymns he penned shortly before his death, the Christian call into the world is this:

> Come to the waters, whoever is thirsty.
> Drink from the fountain that never runs dry.
> Jesus the Living One, offers you mercy,
> Life more abundant in boundless supply.
>
> Come to the Savior, the God of salvation.
> God has provided an end to sin's strife.
> Why will you suffer the Law's condemnation?
> Take the free gift of the water of life.[4]

Two Obstacles to Overcome

We are viewing this as an evangelistic encounter, and as we find, there will always be obstacles that keep people from God. Our passage shows two of them, beginning with *the problem of sin*. Jesus shows us that our witness to the gospel must squarely confront people with the reality and consequences of sin. People must be convicted of their sin if they are to accept the gospel, because the salvation it proclaims is from sin and its guilt.

It is no surprise that Jesus should press the matter of this woman's sin, for it was sin he came to overcome and remove. The Samaritan woman, however, was not thinking this way, and the reason was her lack of concern for sin. Her only reply to his offer was this: "Sir, give me this water so that I won't get thirsty and have to keep coming here to draw water" (John 4:15). It is hard to tell if she was being sarcastic or not. She would be glad not to have to walk back to this well over and over. She thought of Jesus as a plumber and not as a Savior, because she saw only her physical need for water. Not realizing that her true need was forgiveness for sin and a new power for life, she, like many today, failed to see the point of Jesus' offer.

But Jesus' response changed the tune quickly enough: "Go, call your husband and come back." "I have no husband," she replied (John 4:16–17). Jesus responded that she had no husband because she was living with a man out of wedlock, having run through five husbands before.

The conviction of sin is an essential goal of all true Christian proclamation. If we are going to do any good to people's souls, then we must bring them to see themselves as God sees them—as guilty transgressors. Scripture teaches that "all have sinned and fall short of the glory of God" (Rom. 3:23). That is true of everyone, not just scandalous people like this woman.

Jesus was obviously determined that the salvation he offered not be disassociated from the necessary forgiveness of sin. And it is evident from what happened that he hit his mark. "Jesus said to her, 'You are right when you say you have no husband. The fact is, you have had five husbands, and the man you now have is not your husband. What you have just said is quite true.' 'Sir,' the woman said, 'I can see that you are a prophet'" (John 4:17–19). Then, perhaps to change the subject but also perhaps because she was reminded of the need to offer sacrifices to God, she turned the conversation to the matter of religious controversy. "Our fathers worshiped on this mountain, but you Jews claim that the place where we must worship is in Jerusalem" (John 4:20).

I said that there are two obstacles between people and God, the first of which is sin. The second is *ignorance*. This woman was ignorant of true and saving religion. Like other Samaritans, she had been taught that Mount Gerizim, near where they stood, was the place where the Lord was to be sought. This is what she brought up to Jesus, the main religious dispute between Samaritans and Jews, whether or not this mountain or Mount Zion in Jerusalem was the proper place to worship God.

Samaritans did not accept any of the Old Testament except the five books of Moses, Genesis to Deuteronomy. Having rejected so much of God's revelation, it is no wonder they worshiped him falsely. True worship is always based on what God has established in his Word. In the days of the old covenant, God's Word stipulated Jerusalem as the proper place for his worship. The Samaritans instead worshiped on this mountain in their land.

All this shows the extent of her ignorance, which was a great barrier to her salvation. Notice Jesus' response. He affirms the matter of truth—it is the Jews who were right and not the Samaritans. "You Samaritans worship what you do not know; we worship what we do know, for salvation is from the Jews" (John 4:22). The right answer did matter. But Jesus came not to give victory to the Jews over the Samaritans but to be the Savior for Jews and Samaritans alike. Therefore he points to his saving work and its implications. "A time is coming," he says, "and has now come when the true worshipers will worship the Father in spirit and truth" (v. 23). Now that he has come, as a result of the ministry he would perform, the situation has changed. Location is no longer essential to worship. All that Mount Zion stood for, all that the temple in Jerusalem signified, was fulfilled in the coming of Jesus Christ so that true worship now is in him. He is the Way to God, and he is the Truth of God incarnate.

This point completes Jesus' evangelistic example. First, he treated this woman with dignity, asking of her a service and thereby gaining a hearing. Second, he used the setting to direct her to spiritual realities. Third, he did not avoid but confronted the reality of sin, and then, fourth, he dealt with the problem of ignorance by setting forth his saving work, which is the focus of all true evangelism.

"I Am He"

Jesus pointed out to the woman that the answer to her question was not a place but a person. He spoke of a time that was to come, and now was dawning, when worship would be defined not by place but by character. "A time is coming and has now come when the true worshipers will worship the Father in spirit and truth, for they are the kind of worshipers the Father seeks. God is spirit, and his worshipers must worship in spirit and in truth" (John 4:23–24). That is a teaching worthy of many sermons. Let me observe that true worship does not take place simply when we seat ourselves in an appropriate place for an hour or two but only when we spiritually meet with God, praising him for all that he is and all he has done for us in Jesus Christ, and when we do so on the basis of the truth he has revealed in Scripture. That is what God seeks from us, true worship as defined by him. It is true spiritual worship empowered by the work of his Holy Spirit through faith in Jesus.

Most important is what happens in John 4:25–26. Jesus gained this woman's attention when he revealed his knowledge of her sin. Then he spoke of the reality of spiritual fellowship with God, something she obviously had never known before. All she could do was express her hope in the Messiah who was to come. "When he comes," she feebly replied, "he will explain everything to us." It was then that Jesus closed his case, moving forward to the revelation he had intended all along. "I who speak to you," he said, "am he."

In the Greek text this is simply "I am." Jesus declared, "I am—he is speaking to you." Those words would have been eminently familiar to a woman whose entire Bible consisted of the books written by Moses. "I am" is what God said to Moses at the burning bush, when the Lord revealed his name to the deliverer:

> Moses said to God, "Suppose I go to the Israelites and say to them, 'The God of your fathers has sent me to you,' and they ask me, 'What is his name?' Then what shall I tell them?" God said to Moses, "I AM WHO I AM. This is what you are to say to the Israelites: 'I AM has sent me to you.'" (Exod. 3:13–14)

By identifying himself with this name, "I AM," Jesus is revealing that he is the Lord and the God of Moses, that here with him is holy ground no less than was the ground before the burning bush. Here was the true revelation of God, as Jesus says later in this Gospel: "I and the Father are one" (John 10:30), and "Anyone who has seen me has seen the Father" (John 14:9).

Do you see the point? God is no longer revealing himself only in faraway corners like Mount Sinai, only to his select people like Moses. The great "I AM," the God of Israel and of the Old Testament, has come up the road to Samaria and sat down at a well and revealed himself to a sinful woman of an outcast tribe. Like God to Moses at the burning bush, Jesus here calls this woman into his service, to lead her people out in an exodus of salvation. This is what Jesus meant in John 4:23: "Believe me, woman, a time is coming when you will worship the Father neither on this mountain nor in Jerusalem." Why? Because the location of God's saving presence in the world is wherever Jesus is, wherever he is preached and believed. Therefore William Cowper is right to have us sing:

> Jesus, where'er thy people meet,
> There they behold thy mercy seat;
> Where'er they seek thee, thou art found,
> And ev'ry place is hallowed ground.

The ground on which we worship is Jesus Christ, who says, "I am the way and the truth and the life. No one comes to the Father except through me" (John 14:6). That is what Jesus was doing in this world, revealing God, bringing God out beyond the confines of Jerusalem, having fulfilled the law and then ushered in the age of grace and truth. He called this sinful woman to be the Moses of Sychar, and he is calling men and woman everywhere into his service today.

Savior of the World

I said at the beginning that truth is stranger and more marvelous than fiction. What could be more marvelous than this! This sinful, cynical woman has met God in the flesh. Her ignorance and her sin have been removed by the Savior of the world, and she races off to serve as his evangelist to her people. John 4:28–29 tells us, "Then, leaving her water jar, the woman went back to the town and said to the people, 'Come, see a man who told me everything I ever did. Could this be the Christ?'"

Surely this detail about the water jug being left behind is included for emphasis. She left her water jar, having evidently found a stream of living water and thus forgetting the well to which she first had come. She was no longer thirsty but bubbling forth with a fountain of life, and what she did next bears the stamp of saving faith. As John Calvin writes, "It is the nature of faith that we want to bring others to share eternal life with us when we have become partakers of it."[5] By John 4:39 we find many of the Samaritans believing on Jesus because of her testimony, so that Jesus stayed with them two days while more became disciples. They saw him with their eyes and heard him with their ears, and they declared, "We know that this man really is the Savior of the world" (v. 42).

All that is strange and marvelous, but there is something stranger and more marvelous still. Namely, that this still happens today when people find themselves before the same living God, like Moses at the bush and this woman at the well, as the gospel is preached and read.

What then should you do when you encounter the living God in the person of Christ and in his gospel? The Bible says, in its last chapter, " 'Come!' And let him who hears say, 'Come!' Whoever is thirsty, let him come; and whoever wishes, let him take the free gift of the water of life" (Rev. 22:17). Jesus said to the woman, and he says to you, "If you knew the gift of God, you would ask him, and he will give you living water." Ask and you will receive, even the springing waters of eternal life. And then he will give you a purpose in life such as you never have had. He will make you, like this woman, a bearer of that same living water for the souls of a thirsty world, so that many will hear and be saved.

Jesus and the Man by the Pool

John 5:1–15

Then Jesus said to him, "Get up! Pick up your mat and walk." At once the man was cured; he picked up his mat and walked. The day on which this took place was a Sabbath.
(John 5:8–9)

During a recent summer, Philadelphia was graced by the presence of tall ships from the bygone age of sailing, as part of its Independence Day celebrations. Those sailing vessels are a sight of singular beauty. But they also remind me of one of the most helpful illustrations I have ever heard regarding the Christian life. A sailing ship needs two things in order to move in a proper direction. The same is true of us. First, the ship needs a rudder, which points it in the

Outpouring or House of Mercy. John's description of the place is found in John 5:2: "Now there is in Jerusalem near the Sheep Gate a pool, which in Aramaic is called Bethesda and which is surrounded by five covered colonnades." This place has been uncovered by archaeologists, so that we now know that it was an area with twin pools, surrounded on all sides by these covered porches and with one in between, which accounts for the five colonnades.[2]

What is important, however, is not the architecture but the human tragedy that unfolded before the eyes of our Lord. There were, John writes, "a great number of disabled people." The Greek word used to give this general description, *astheneia*, is most commonly translated as "weak." The New American Standard version has it as "sick," while the King James says "impotent." Other translations are "helpless," "infirm," "powerless," or "feeble." James Montgomery Boice, in his commentary on John, sums up the significance of what this verse describes:

> This is the human race as it stands apart from the grace of God through Jesus Christ. How does God view men before that act in which he places new life within them? The one answer is in Romans 5:6, which tells us that it was when we were "yet without strength" that Christ died for the "ungodly." . . . In other words, God tells us that it was when we found it impossible to do anything for ourselves spiritually that Christ died for us.[3]

When we speak of spiritual inability, however, it is important for us to make clear what we mean. It is not true that we are unable to obey God, to trust him or serve him or worship him in an absolute sense. Indeed, we were created with these duties specifically in mind, and this potential is central to our identity. This is mainly what it means when the Bible tells us that we were created "in the image of God" (Gen. 1:26). Therefore our failure to believe and obey God is never excused on the basis of inability.

With that in mind, the Scripture teaches that man in his fallen state is gripped by a spiritual inability borne of sin. The two doctrines that deal with this problem are original sin and total depravity. Original sin is not so much an event as a condition. It reflects on something that happened, namely, our first parents' sin against God in the garden, but more specifically it points to the effect of that sin as it pertains to us, to our condition as its result. John Calvin is right when he says, "All of us tend to evil, and we are not only inclined to it, but we are, as it were, boiling hot with it."[4] Genesis 6:5 speaks to this when it describes why God brought the first great judgment in Noah's flood: "The LORD saw how great man's wickedness on the earth had become, and that every inclination of the thoughts of his heart was only evil all the time." The apostle Paul writes in Ephesians 2:3 that all of us are "by nature objects of wrath." Psalm 51:5 says, "Surely I was sinful at birth," or as the King James Version more eloquently puts it, "Behold, I was shapen in iniquity; and in sin did my mother conceive me." Original sin means that we are sinners not because we have sinned but because our first parents sinned, as shown in Genesis 3. We have inherited their corrupt natures and their guilt, as Paul demonstrates in Romans 5:12–21. We sin, therefore, because we are sinners by nature, and not the other way around.

Because of the condition of original sin we are spiritually disabled, as depicted by these people at the pool of Bethesda. The doctrine of total depravity deals with the extent of this disability. The Bible teaches that sin has corrupted us thoroughly, comprehensively, totally. This does not mean that there is nothing good about us in any way or that we are as bad as we might be. Rather, it affirms the Bible's teaching that there is no part of us, no faculty, that is not corrupted by sin. It is a total, a comprehensive depravity.

The Bible's catalogue of natural corruption runs from top to bottom. Isaiah writes,

> From the sole of your foot to the top of your head
> there is no soundness. (Isa. 1:6)

Included are our hands, which "are full of blood" (Isa. 1:15), our feet, which "rush into sin" (Prov. 1:16), our tongues, which "practice deceit" (Rom. 3:13), our eyes, which are "haughty" (Prov. 21:4), our ears, which are closed and dull of hearing when God is speaking (Isa. 6:10), our minds, which are futile and "darkened in understanding" (Eph. 4:18), and our hearts. Especially our hearts are corrupt! Jeremiah says,

> The heart is deceitful above all things
> and beyond cure.
> Who can understand it? (Jer. 17:9)

This is why we need God's Word, and especially God's law. We need to be pointed in a right direction. Being totally depraved, our conscience is not a reliable guide. Our judgment and our desires are not trustworthy. We are blind, like many of the disabled people at this pool, and cannot see our way.

But we need more than God's law, more than a true

course set upon the wheel of our ship. Why? Because we, like the others at the pool, are lame and paralyzed. We do not possess the power to move ourselves along the right azimuth any more than a sailing ship can sail without wind buffeting its canvas. Without the power that comes from God through the gospel we are not able to follow even a right course but are stuck interminably in the doldrums of our sin.

Religion's Failure

That is what this scene Christ encountered at the pool so well illustrates: the blind and the lame, those disabled and lacking all ability to save themselves. But there is one man in particular Jesus encounters:

> One who was there had been an invalid for thirty-eight years. When Jesus saw him lying there and learned that he had been in this condition for a long time, he asked him, "Do you want to get well?" "Sir," the invalid replied, "I have no one to help me into the pool when the water is stirred. While I am trying to get in, someone else goes down ahead of me." (John 5:5–7)

If we ask what brought Jesus to this encounter, the answer is simple. He is the great Physician, and so he sought out the sick. If we ask why the man was there, the answer is equally obvious. He was terribly needy and desperate for healing power. He is like so many people today. They are desperately looking for power, and well they should. Some are looking for power to heal the afflictions of their body, but a great many more are seeking a power to heal their soul. Our society is a veritable factory of candidates for this pool at Bethesda—those abandoned and rejected, those abused and afflicted, the lonely and broken and warped in heart and in spirit. They are all around us, many of them appearing quite whole. But they are not. And they are desperately seeking power. They should be.

But, you may reply, this man is looking at the wrong place. His idea of healing from this pool is pure superstition. He believes, as John 5:7 tells us, that when the water of this pool is stirred, the first one in will be healed. You may notice that the New International Version excludes John 5:4, which is included in the margin. This verse is missing from the earlier manuscripts and is obviously a later addition, no doubt to convey the popular belief about this pool. It says, "From time to time an angel of the Lord would come down and stir up the waters. The first one in the pool after each such disturbance would be cured of whatever disease he had." That is rightly removed from the Bible's text, but it gives us a good sense of what this man believed.

I have no doubt that this pool had some restorative powers, or else this kind of superstition could not have been attached to it. But the religion of the Bible is never a vague mysticism, never a superstitious manipulation of divine powers, but a religion of worship and faith in a God of grace and might. It is to God we are to look, not to pools or ancient artifacts or images of Mary, all of which is pure idolatry. These are the very things the first commandment warns against. This poor man would have better spent his time at the temple beseeching God for mercy than waiting at this pool.

And yet, if we know something about the Old Testament religion as it had been warped and corrupted in the time of Jesus, then we understand why this man turned to find power in the superstitious reputation of this pool of water. The Jews of that day are well represented in this passage, and what they represent is the lifelessness, the powerlessness of a dead formalism.

This is a text that has received a great deal of allegorical interpretation, most of it linking this pool with the futility of the Old Testament law. In these allegories, the five colonnades stand for the five books of Moses, the thirty-eight years the man had been at the pool line up with Israel's thirty-eight years of unnecessary wandering in the desert, and the waters stand for the tabernacle system for cleansing. William Barclay summarizes the point of these comparisons: "In the porches the people lay ill. The law could show a man his sin, but could never mend it; the law could uncover a man's weakness, but could never cure it. The law, like the porches, sheltered the sick soul but could never heal it."[5]

That kind of extensive allegory probably reads a bit more into John's text than it takes out. But there is, I think, something to it. For one thing, it is well established that John 6–8 employ a strong exodus motif, with the themes of manna, water flowing from the rock, and God's light leading his people. The thirty-eight years of this man's waiting, here in chapter 5, may well anticipate that thematic connection. Furthermore, there is an ongoing comparison in John's Gospel between what is symbolized by water and that which Christ ushers in by his saving work and power. In John 2, Jesus' first miracle was the changing of water into wine. Indeed, it was not just water, but, as verse 6 says, "the kind used by the Jews for ceremonial washing," that is, for the rites of the law. Wine, in contrast to lifeless water, is a frequent metaphor for the bounteous blessings of the new age in Christ (see Mark

2:22). Again, in John 4, where the encounter takes place on the well built by Jacob, that is, the father of Israel, Jesus says, "Everyone who drinks this water will be thirsty again, but whoever drinks the water I give him will never thirst" (John 4:13–14).

This is not a condemnation of the Old Testament and its religion, for the Old Testament anticipates and relies upon the coming work of Jesus Christ. But what it does condemn is any religion, and certainly the Jewish religion of Christ's time, when it is made into a performance-based, ritualistic tradition devoid of the power of God's grace. The futility of such religion is not something we see in the lives of Moses or David or the other great Old Testament figures, who eagerly looked forward to the Messiah and drew hope and power from God. But it is the empty formalism we see in the rulers and Pharisees of Jesus' day.

It was the latter that drove this poor invalid to spend nearly four decades waiting for something to happen, waiting for something of life to bring him power. How many others had waited on and on without ever seeing anything of real hope and power? How many today are searching and seeking, going from this fad to that program, from this methodology to that ritual, from one experience and excitement to another, all without ever encountering anything truly divine? Like this man at this pool, unless Jesus comes and enters into our situation, nothing with real and saving power from God is present.

This passage gives a most telling condemnation of formal externalism, and it does so through the religious leaders who responded to Jesus' healing of this man. After Jesus called him to his feet and the man set off with his mat upon his back, they came to him saying, "It is the Sabbath; the law forbids you to carry your mat" (John 5:10). The man replied that the one who performed the miracle told him to do this. "So they asked him, 'Who is this fellow who told you to pick it up and walk?'" (John 5:12).

This is remarkable in the extreme. Here is a man who had been lame for thirty-eight years, who has been healed by miraculous power, and this is of no interest to the leaders of formal, external religion. Their concern does not lie in the healing of the sick, in the uplifting of the downcast, in the strengthening of the weak. They are not stimulated by the presence of a blatant miracle but only by a violation of their agenda and program. They do not praise God for so great a miracle. Their whole interest is absorbed in their restrictions and rules. Their whole interest is disclosed in the words, "It is the Sabbath; the law forbids you to carry your mat."

There is a great warning to us all, and especially to those like myself who serve as leaders in religion. When our focus is on our empires, our agenda, our program, and not on the blessing of God in the lives of spiritually and physically downcast people, then we have crossed a terrible line, one that separated Jesus from his religious opponents. Unless we rejoice at the salvation of a single sinner, then our hearts are out of tune with the music that is of heaven; unless we weep with those in sorrow and laugh with those in joy, then we have followed a different pattern from the one we see in Jesus.

For the record, the Old Testament law did not forbid a man to carry his mat on the Sabbath. It forbade work on the Sabbath. The rabbis took it upon themselves to spell out what qualified as work. They produced thirty-nine classes of work, including the bearing of burdens from one place to another. This man, however, was hardly carrying his mat in an occupational capacity. This was not a worldly pursuit that secularized the Sabbath. But in the interests of their agenda, their tradition, these religious formalists had lost sight of the real meaning of the Sabbath, namely, God's blessing upon man, which is what Christ came to give.

This example of formal externalism serves to represent every religious system, every spiritual methodology devoid of life from God through Jesus Christ, even if it calls itself Christian. We may say the same thing about formal ritual-ists as about those who reject all tradition in a frenzied pur-suit of informality and spontaneity. It does not matter whether you are following a New Age guru, reading self-help psychology, venerating Mary and the saints, pursuing some religious method and discipline, or endangering your soul at the occultist's shop. Unless Jesus Christ has come into your life as he did upon the scene of this invalid, there is no real power for healing, no light from heaven, no hope for salvation.

Christ's Power to Save

We have seen how the leaders of empty religion have treated this man. He is not of real interest to them, and they regard him as a nothing, in the same way that worldly religion sees men and women today as tools, as marketing opportunities, as sources of revenue and influence. But no-tice the difference when we turn to Jesus.

It is striking that our Lord did not reprove this man for the folly stretching back many years, no doubt, of waiting and watching for a miracle at this pool. Jesus might well have rebuked him for his practical idolatry, seeking aid from a pool rather than crying out in prayer to God. But Je-sus saw and knew the desperation within this man, an in-valid for thirty-eight years. Out of his boundless mercy he

asked, "Do you want to get well?" This is how Jesus handled
the lost and the lame, the needy sheep scattered and without a shepherd, and it is the kind of mercy this confused
and needy world needs from Christians today.

Jesus said three things to the man by the pool, each of
which is highly significant. First, he asked him, "Do you
want to get well?" (John 5:6). That is Jesus' interest in this
world, and it is this that he offers in earnest to a world so
well depicted by the scene at this pool. He came to give
sight to the blind: "I have come into the world as a light, so
that no one who believes in me should stay in darkness"
(John 12:46). And he came to lift up the weak and the
weary, the hopeless and the lost. "For God did not send his
Son into the world to condemn the world, but to save the
world through him" (John 3:17). Therefore it is Jesus that
you need. Not a superstitious angle. Not a method or a program, be it mystical or moral. Not religion itself. It is Jesus
to whom we are called; it is Jesus who is the Answer sent
from God. "I am the way and the truth and the life. No one
comes to the Father except through me" (John 14:6), he
declares.

The second thing Jesus said to this man proved this
point. John 5:8–9 tells us, "Then Jesus said to him, 'Get up!
Pick up your mat and walk.' At once the man was cured; he
picked up his mat and walked." That is power, and it stands
for the whole of what Jesus can do, body and soul, to those
who look to him in faith. Later on, when the religious leaders accosted him for healing on the Sabbath, Jesus referred
to this healing: "For just as the Father raises the dead and
gives them life, even so the Son gives life to whom he is
pleased to give it" (John 5:21). The word for "raising" the
dead in John 5:21 is the same as the word in Jesus' command in John 5:8, "Get up!" This seems to make the point

that just as God raises the dead, he has given to Jesus the power that he in turn may give to people like this invalid. It is the same power of God that raised Jesus from the dead that Jesus wields when he speaks, to raise others from their despair and defeat. Jesus' call is effectual and saving because it is the call of God.

We see the power of Christ's call and command all through the Gospel accounts. Jesus came to Matthew at the tax collector's booth, where the future apostle was sitting in his sin. "Follow me," he called, "and Matthew got up and followed him" (Matt. 9:9). Jesus stood before the tomb of Lazarus, who had been dead for four days. "Lazarus, come out!" he cried, and "the dead man came out." You see the point. It is Christ who calls you out of sin and death, with the power of God and of life. This is how sinners are saved even today, by the voice of Christ in the gospel. Jesus said to the invalid, "Get up!" and the lame man got up and walked. Note the sovereignty he displays in all this saving grace. "You did not choose me," he told his disciples, "but I chose you and appointed you to go and bear fruit" (John 15:16).

All of that is great good news, because this man had never been able to do what now he did, had never risen and taken up his mat, until the power of Christ gave him the strength. Christ's power went forth with his call and cast the invalid out of the doldrums, as it were, and sent him sailing as he never could have done on his own. This is how conversion works, when first we believe and are saved. It is Christ's power that enables us to believe. That is also how it works all through our Christian lives. His Word gives us strength we lack in ourselves, resurrection power for spiritually vibrant lives. "Apart from me," he told the disciples, "you can do nothing" (John 15:5). Without Christ there is no spiritual power, but with Christ we have the power that raised him from the grave. This is what the apostle Paul wrote of in his great prayer for believers in Ephesians 1:18–20:

> I pray also that the eyes of your heart may be enlightened in order that you may know the hope to which he has called you, the riches of his glorious inheritance in the saints, and his incomparably great power for us who believe. That power is like the working of his mighty strength, which he exerted in Christ when he raised him from the dead.

That is what we see in Jesus' simple but sublime words, "Get up! Pick up your mat and walk."

Finally, Jesus went to this man sometime later when he was at the temple. I take that as a good sign. This man was not discouraged by the legalistic tyrants of formal religion but had gone to the temple, no doubt to pray and worship God with his newfound strength. Jesus said to him, "See, you are well again. Stop sinning or something worse may happen to you" (John 5:14). Jesus had not healed him, had not given him new strength, so he could go on to a life of sin. Jesus heals for the sake of righteousness, so that his Father's will might be done on earth as in heaven. Jesus' intention was that those he saved should lead new and godly lives. He said to his disciples in John 15:16, "I chose you and appointed you to go and bear fruit—fruit that will last."

Many commentators conclude from this last statement of Jesus to this man that his disability had been caused by some earlier sin or that his heart was still in bondage to iniquity. I am not so sure, and I find it difficult to make definite statements about his spiritual state with so little evidence. But his presence at the temple and his willingness to put his trust in Jesus' command seem to be evidence of at least a budding faith.

This much is clear from what Jesus says, that Christians are saved not only from the consequences of sin but also from the life of sin. "See, you are well again," he says, and adds, "Stop sinning." Yes, we are saved from the law's condemnation. We are saved by grace and not by our attainments. But we are saved to be keepers of God's law as it is the expression of his character and will. Our obedience in this life, by faith in Christ, makes a difference now and in the future, when our works will be judged, even though we ourselves are saved and forgiven (see 1 Cor. 3:12–15).

Earlier we considered the illustration of the sailing ship to the Christian life, and here it is helpful again. The ship has a rudder that directs it, just as we have many commandments in Scripture, which we categorize as law. What it needs is the wind to fill its sails, just as we need the grace of Christ to give us his energizing power through the gospel. What Jesus is telling this man, in terms of this illustration, is that if he expects to arrive in the port of heaven, then the rudder and the sails will have to work in combination to lead him in paths of righteousness. If they do not, things will be far worse for him than ever before. The same is true for us. We are saved by grace alone through faith alone, but that grace and that faith never are alone. They are accompanied by a life of good works and a turning from sin that is ever the sign of true salvation. As Arthur Pink observes, "Renewed health ought to send us back into the world with a greater hatred of sin, a more thorough watchfulness over our ways, a greater determination to live for God's glory."[6]

We hear no more of this once-enfeebled man after this one encounter. But the last word on him in our passage is an encouraging one. Jesus told him to sin no more, and although we are not told how he subsequently lived, we have this statement from John 5:15: "The man went away and told the Jews that it was Jesus who had made him well." That was the truth. It is Jesus alone who heals our sin-sick souls; it is he alone who makes us ultimately well. And the best good work we ever can do is to tell others this great and saving truth, hoping that they too will look to him for their salvation.

Jesus and the Woman Caught in Adultery

John 7:53–8:11

Jesus straightened up and asked her, "Woman, where are they? Has no one condemned you?" "No one, sir," she said. "Then neither do I condemn you," Jesus declared. "Go now and leave your life of sin." (John 8:10–11)

Sometimes we encounter a sin that is so staggering it is disgusting to reflect upon the human condition. The Bible recounts numerous such examples. I think of Pharaoh and later King Herod ordering the murder of infant boys to protect their insecure perch upon a throne. I think of Jezebel and her cold-blooded destruction of innocent Naboth and her subsequent theft of his vineyard, just to provide another bauble for her husband, King Ahab. There is King Jehoiakim cynically carving up the scroll Baruch had lovingly copied for Jeremiah, the scroll with the very words of God, arrogantly discarding each piece into the fire. But even in that company, I know of no sin recorded in all of Scripture so dripping with evil as the one found in this passage from John 8.

I am not referring to adultery. Oh, to be sure, adultery is a great evil. The Ten Commandments condemn it, as did Jesus and as did the apostles after him. If I were to list any one sin that is doing the most damage in our society, it might well be adultery. With the emotional and spiritual damage it does to the participants comes the far vaster toll of broken marriages, fatherless children, and now even deadly disease. Adultery is no small affair. Indeed, I think there are few callings for Christians in a culture such as ours higher than that to sexual purity. Conversely, there are few worse things we can do than commit adultery, which so destroys any Christian witness.

But with all that said, adultery is more a sin of weakness than of malice. Adultery is born of folly and self-indulgence, and those are bad things. But the sin that dominates our passage was constructed out of far worse materials. It was born of malice and arrogance, anger and envy and evil intents. It was a sin in which a woman was used, even offered up for destruction, for the sake of bringing down a man whose message, however true, was inconvenient to others' agenda.

That is the motive behind the events in these verses. As we have been tracking Jesus' encounters with ordinary people in John's Gospel we have been incidentally observing the growing enmity toward him on the part of the religious leaders. In John 2 this began with his cleansing of the temple and their demand to know his authority. In John 5 the resentment ripened into malice, when Jesus was insensitive enough to their religious agenda to heal a desperate man on the day God established for man's blessing, that is, the Sabbath. John told us then, "For this reason the Jews tried all the harder to kill him" (John 5:18).

We have now moved ahead to the end of John 7 and the beginning of John 8. During this time the hatred of these leaders toward Jesus only heightened. When the common people began spreading the word that this Jesus might really be the Christ, the Pharisees and chief priests responded by sending the temple guards to arrest him (John 7:32). How frustrated they must have been when the guards returned empty-handed, having found Jesus but then been overawed by his teaching and presence. When asked why they did not arrest him, the guards answered, "No one ever spoke the way this man does" (John 7:46). In the aftermath of these events, Nicodemus spoke up for Jesus in the Sanhedrin, only to find himself threatened and put down in the assembly for his effort.

A Terrible Conspiracy

Our passage follows immediately on those events. Having failed to arrest our Lord, the scribes and the Pharisees resorted to a clever and sinister trap to discredit him. They must have been pleased with their stratagem, because it is always better to disgrace an enemy than to have his blood upon your hands. It was an evil plan, yes, but it was also a stroke of genius.

Let's consider the evil first. The more we know about ancient Jewish legal procedures, the more clear it becomes that this is not simply a case of callous opportunism toward a sinful woman, but rather that what we have is a conspiracy and a set-up. One thing we must acknowledge about Judaism in the time of Christ is that, when it came to the enforcement of the law, the procedures were extremely careful and judicious. This was particularly true in the case of any crime punishable by execution; the standards of proof were so high that it was almost impossible to secure a conviction. Records from the rabbinical book the Mishnah show that this was intentional and that executions almost never took place (see *Makhoth* 1, 10).

Adultery was one of those crimes punishable by death. Deuteronomy 22:22, as well as Leviticus 20, establishes the crime and the punishment. It was, however, necessary for the couple to be caught engaging in sexual intercourse—it was not enough to find them in an inappropriate or compromising situation—and by multiple witnesses whose testimony agreed to the smallest detail. One scholar who has studied Jewish legal procedures states, "The actual physical movements of the couple must have been capable of no other explanation, and the witnesses must have seen exactly the same acts at exactly the same time, in the presence of each other, so that their depositions would be identical in every respect."[1]

In the apocryphal book Susanna, a woman falsely accused of adultery is acquitted because the witnesses cannot agree on what kind of tree she supposedly committed adultery beneath. You see the level of detail required to obtain a conviction and how hard it would be to produce such a situation unless it was a set-up. The witnesses would have to be in place in advance, with planning and coordination of the details.

Furthermore, we cannot help but notice that the scribes and Pharisees dragged only the woman forward. They say they witnessed the act of adultery, but they did not produce the man. At the least, they let him get away, and the man abandoned the woman to take the fall—which, by the way, is usually how it works out in such cases. But more likely, it seems that the man was in on the plot and engaged in sexual intercourse for the purpose of incriminating this poor woman. This shows a callous attitude about sin and contempt for human life.

This is a despicable plot. It gets worse when we consider their attitude to the Word of God. They treated the law as nothing more than a weapon for trapping Jesus. "Teacher, this woman was caught in the act of adultery. In the Law Moses commanded us to stone such women. Now what do you say?" (John 8:4–5). There was no need for this question. As they state, the law was clear on this point, so the question had only the purpose given in John 8:6: "They were using this question as a trap, in order to have a basis for accusing him." That is an ignoble purpose for the Word of God, to say the least.

Even further, if they were in a position to witness the act of adultery, they surely were in a position to keep the sin from happening. If they wanted to uphold the law, they would have prevented the sin rather than waiting to exploit it. No wonder Jesus called such people "children of the devil" later in this chapter (John 8:44), for this is the very use Satan loves to make of the Bible, twisting it, manipulating God's Word of truth into a weapon in service of sin.

Worst of all was their treatment of this sinful woman, which was brutally indelicate. There was no reason to bring her into public view. Even for the purpose of trapping Jesus, they had only to ask the question hypothetically, without all this public show. But they were eager to sacrifice her if only to add to the drama, if only to heighten the pressure placed upon Jesus. Arthur Pink sums up the situation with these words:

> The awful malignity of the Lord's enemies is evident on the surface. They brought this adulterous woman to Christ not because they were shocked at her conduct, still less because they were grieved that God's holy law had been broken. Their object was to use this woman to exploit her sin and further their own evil designs. With cold-blooded indelicacy they acted, employing the guilt of the captive to accomplish their evil intentions against Christ.[2]

I have mentioned the devilish nature of the Pharisees' action, and when we compare their behavior here with that of Satan we find that is literally true. It is remarkable how similar this episode is to the scene in Zechariah 3:1, where the devil plays this role against a man named Joshua, who was then the high priest of Israel. In his fourth vision, Zechariah says, "Then he showed me Joshua the high priest standing before the angel of the LORD, and Satan standing at his right side to accuse him." In a striking similarity, these Pharisees act out this same dread pageant, with the same motives as the devil before them. It was not a concern for God or for righteousness that motivated them but a manipulative zeal borne of selfishness that led them to accuse this woman.

Before moving on, let me observe that this kind of evil is in us, it is in you, and not just hypothetically. If, for instance, your thoughts could be known, and God does know them, then you would have a long record of wicked crimes of this very sort. It is, as I said, disgusting to gaze upon the human condition as we are in sin.

Finally, we must note the close connection between the hardened condition of these religious leaders and their rejection of Jesus Christ. In Hebrews 6, where the subject of apostasy is discussed, the point is made that those who knowingly reject Jesus Christ run the risk of becoming so hardened that they are beyond repentance (Heb. 6:4–6). In the case of these scribes and Pharisees, despite their outward shows of righteousness, their hatred for Jesus bore fruit in the worst sort of callousness and evil and had the most dreadful effects upon their spiritual condition.

A Serious Dilemma

Such is the evil in this terrible conspiracy. But we have to admit there is also considerable genius at work. Their intention was to discredit Jesus, as John 8:6 tells us, and this situation they brought before him was suitably crafted to that end.

Consider the options presented to our Lord. On the one hand, he could counsel the forgiveness of this woman's sin. That would seem consistent with his preaching of grace, but at the expense of setting aside the law. That would greatly discredit Jesus' ministry and undermine his credibility. God is holy and burns against sin. Anyone who brushed aside the demands of his justice would not be credible as a divine messenger.

On the other hand, Jesus could take his stand with Moses, calling for the condemnation of this woman. But that would be at the expense of his teaching of grace. John Calvin put it succinctly, "Their intention was to force Christ to give up his office of preaching grace, so that he might seem fickle and unsteady."[3] John 3:17 says, "For God did not send his Son into the world to condemn the world, but to save the world through him." Christ, to stand with the law, would have to give up that mission—a great loss indeed.

Imagine Jesus saying, "Yes, this woman is guilty and must be punished. You should gather stones and put her to death. Then, should you happen upon the man, his fate must be the same." If Jesus had said that, what sinner would ever come weeping to his feet? What poor wretch, overcome by the flesh and temptation, in sorrow for sin and for guilt, would ever dare go to Jesus for help, either then or today? Such a person must conclude, "No, this Jesus is a condemner of sinners. He will give me up to judgment and punishment, even up to death." Pink expresses the problem well:

> The problem presented to Christ by His enemies was no mere local one. So far as human reason can perceive it was the profoundest moral problem which ever could or can confront God Himself. That problem was how justice and mercy could be harmonized. . . . How can mercy be exercised when the sword of justice bars her way? How can grace flow forth except by slighting holiness?[4]

Jesus' Mastery and Mercy

It is against the backdrop of this terrible conspiracy, this cunning trap, that Jesus reveals his mastery over every circumstance. Jesus, we have seen, was in a dilemma, and his response was remarkable, if somewhat puzzling. John tells us this:

> Jesus bent down and started to write on the ground with his finger. When they kept on questioning

him, he straightened up and said to them, "If any one of you is without sin, let him be the first to throw a stone at her." Again he stooped down and wrote on the ground. (John 8:6–8)

It is impossible for us to know for sure what Jesus wrote on the ground, or even what he meant by this action. The commentators make numerous suggestions. Some say he was listing the sins of the accusers in the dirt, others that he was writing out his response before speaking it, as Roman judges did when rendering a verdict, still others that he was writing out the law's condemnations against false witnesses, or the words of Jeremiah 17:13, which say, "O LORD . . . those who turn away from you will be written in the dust." Those are all reasonable suggestions, but I think we have to admit that we don't know more than what John tells us.

But there is something we do know, and that is that Jesus' personal presence deterred these men from their terrible course. The key was his challenge, "If any one of you is without sin, let him be the first to throw a stone at her." With those words he effectively diffused the trap and put the accusers to flight. That statement could not be construed as setting aside the law. At the same time, it protected the woman from harm, since none dared take up his challenge.

It is unclear whether Jesus meant that only one who is completely sinless could execute punishment for sin or that they must be innocent of the particular sin this woman was accused of, a violation of the seventh commandment. At the least his words reminded them that the law demanded that the witnesses were to cast the first stones (Deut. 17:7), and those witnesses had to be free from any association with the crime. Most importantly, however, Jesus lifted the discussion from the legal, from the procedural, to the moral level, and there these wicked men could not stand. Jesus always raises the bar from form to substance, from outward show to inward reality, with the effect that every pretense of self-righteousness stands no chance before him. What was true for these men is true for us as well.

In the glaring presence of the Son of God, these wicked men lacked the gall to press onward, to cast the stone. Just as the guards had drawn back, unwilling to arrest him; just as the soldiers would later fall to their faces when they came with Judas to seize him in the garden (John 18:6), so too did these men fall back from the One who is the Lord. John's account is no doubt understated, "At this, those who heard began to go away, one at a time, the older ones first, until only Jesus was left, with the woman still standing there" (John 8:9). As James Montgomery Boice observes in his commentary:

> Obviously, there was something in the gaze of the Lord Jesus Christ, or in the tone of his voice, or simply in the power of his presence that got through to these men, unrepentant as they were, and left them powerless. Think of the efforts they had gone through! Think of the plotting! Yet they were destroyed in a moment when they were confronted by the God who masters circumstances.[5]

Jesus' words to these wicked men do not mean that there can never be any justice on the human level. They do not mean that no jury can ever condemn a criminal since the members are not perfectly sinless themselves. As Calvin observes, Christ is not forbidding sinners "to do their duty in correcting the sins of others. But by this word, he only reproves hypocrites, who gently flatter themselves and their own vices, but are excessively severe and even savage judges of others."[6] We are, however, put in mind of the merciful attitude we as forgiven sinners must show to others who have sinned; as Jesus taught us, we must pray, "Forgive us our debts, as we have forgiven our debtors" (Matt. 6:12).

Mercy and Justice Kiss

There is the greatest contrast in Jesus' manner of treating this sinful woman compared with the way the scribes and the Pharisees dealt with her. It is always sad to find people using God's Word not to proclaim grace and truth for salvation but to destroy people in order to advance their petty agenda. We found this in our last study of the man beside the pool, and we find plenty of it in our time as well.

But Jesus never treats people as tools, never as mere things. Just as he had done with Nicodemus, then with the woman by the well, and again with the poor desperate invalid by the pool, Jesus deals with people as individuals with significance. His behavior is always marked by care, consideration, and dignity. Jesus treats us as individuals because he has real understanding of what is going on in individual lives. He sees behind the pretense and behind the shame. Our passage again proves the truth of John 2:24–25, "He knew all men. He did not need man's testimony about man, for he knew what was in a man." Jesus shows this understanding as he deals with this woman. He was not naïve about her sin, but neither was he cynical or cold. As Psalm 103:14 says,

> He knows how we are formed,
>   he remembers that we are dust.

Jesus understands men and women in sin, and he understood this woman as an individual.

Second, Jesus showed compassion for her desperate condition. Jesus always looks with compassion on the lost. As Mark tells us from an earlier occasion, "When he saw the crowds, he had compassion on them, because they were harassed and helpless, like sheep without a shepherd" (Mark 9:36). That compassion is born of his great love, a love that neither has nor needs an explanation but is of his nature. "God is love," says 1 John 4:8, and Jesus came to reveal that God and that love to the world.

Therefore Jesus extended forgiveness to the sinful woman. There he was in the sudden quiet of the temple courts, the accusers having fled one by one. Standing up before her, Jesus asked, " 'Woman, where are they? Has no one condemned you?' 'No one, Lord,' she said. 'Then neither do I condemn you,' Jesus declared" (John 8:10–11).

It occurs to me that Jesus might have avoided the trap set for him without going out of his way to save this woman. When they asked him to choose between justice and mercy, he might well have referred them to the Sanhedrin, the body entrusted with such matters. Had Jesus replied, "This is an obvious trap. You are the teachers of the law; you don't need my help for such a matter," I think he would have been safe enough. But to do that would have been to forfeit this woman's life; it would have been to stand still while an injustice was perpetrated. Even if she was guilty, this was not justice. Yes, Jesus was concerned for justice and mercy, and both of them guided his actions in this case. In driving away these evil conspirators, he served the cause of both.

I said earlier that we cannot know what Jesus wrote on the ground. But I think we can know something of why Jesus stooped in this way. This is only suggestive, but I think it is also illuminating. I believe Jesus stooped to the ground not to avoid looking at the accusers but at the accused. He did respect, even love, God's justice in the law, but he had different plans for fulfilling it than through the condemnation of this woman. Therefore he did not turn to her until the law, with its witnesses, had been driven from the scene. Only when they were gone and the law had been disabled did he turn to her, saying, "Woman, where are your accusers?" The apostle Paul writes, "The power of sin is the law" (1 Cor. 15:56), and Jesus waited to deal with her only after the power of sin had been diffused through the removal of the law.

That is the grace Jesus extends to this woman, and it is the heart of the gospel he proclaims. Jesus came not to condemn but to save; he says to this woman and to every sinner who comes to him for mercy, "Neither do I condemn you." And yet we might ask how Christ can proclaim forgiveness when God's holy justice demands judgment. That was the dilemma these men tried to trap him with. So we ask, on what basis does Jesus, on behalf of a just and holy God, say the words "Neither do I condemn you"?

The answer is the cross, toward which Jesus was heading, upon which he would die for the sins of people like this woman. He said to Nicodemus, in John 3:14–15: "Just as Moses lifted up the snake in the desert, so the Son of Man must be lifted up, that everyone who believes in him may have eternal life." That is a reference to the cross, where Jesus took the sin of this woman, took her adulterous guilt upon his innocent back, and put away her sin so that he might speak these words: "Neither do I condemn you."

Jesus speaks forgiveness to us not because we are not guilty and not because God winks at our sin. Jesus is not disinterested in justice; far from it, it was the work of his life and his death. Jesus can say, "Neither do I condemn you," because he has driven off the accusers, having borne their malice himself, having taken the guilt of sin in our place beneath the wrath of God's holy justice. It is the cross that solves the dilemma between justice and mercy, to the glory of God in the highest. It is there at Calvary that Psalm 85:10 can be spoken: "Mercy and truth are met together; righteousness and peace have kissed each other" (KJV).

I said before that I know of no sin more evil than the one this passage shows us, but of course there is one more evil, when the innocent Prince of Peace was put to death at the hands of wicked men. That was the darkest sin, the most evil crime. But just as Christ mastered the plot against this woman caught in adultery, so also God the Father mastered the crime that was his death. God employed it as the instrument of our forgiveness, the reconciliation between his holy justice and his mercy born of love.

Sin Taken Away

I have mentioned the similarity between this episode and the vision presented in Zechariah 3:1. There, Joshua stood in filthy clothes before the angel of the Lord, who represented the Lord Jesus Christ in that vision. At Joshua's right hand was Satan, accusing him for his sin. That vision goes on to show the Lord rebuking the devil, just as Jesus chased off these accusers, and afterward speaking words of marvelous grace:

> The LORD said to Satan, "The LORD rebuke you, Satan! The LORD, who has chosen Jerusalem, rebuke you! Is not this man a burning stick snatched from

the fire?" Now Joshua was dressed in filthy clothes as he stood before the angel. The angel said to those who were standing before him, "Take off his filthy clothes." Then he said to Joshua, "See, I have taken away your sin, and I will put rich garments on you." (Zech. 3:2–4)

That is the great message of the gospel of Jesus Christ, that through faith our sins have been taken away and forgiven. There is, as Paul writes in Romans 8:1, "now no condemnation for those who are in Christ Jesus." This was the good news given as advance warning in John 1:17: "For the law was given through Moses; grace and truth came through Jesus Christ."

Jesus does not stand opposed to the law. He saves us not by despising it but by fulfilling it, by achieving its demands and exhausting its curse. He therefore redeems us to a life of obedience to God, which entails forsaking sin. The law, which once was over our heads as a threat, is now under our feet as a path and guide. In Zechariah's vision, the forgiven man is clothed in white and thenceforth he should sin no more. This is the attitude Jesus displays in his last words to this woman: "Then neither do I condemn you. Go now and leave your life of sin" (John 8:11).

We must never forget this connection, forgiveness of sin that we might in turn forsake sin in obedience to God. But we must also never confuse the order of the two. Jesus does not say, "Leave your life of sin and I will think about forgiving you." Were that the case he might just as well condemn us all now. No, he forgives us on the basis of his own righteous life and sacrificial death. It is by dying on the cross that he takes away our sin, and it is in his perfect righteousness that he clothes us once and for all. As Paul writes in Titus 3:5, "He saved us, not because of righteous things we had done, but because of his mercy." Therefore, if Jesus declares you not condemned, you shall not be charged in the court of God. He will say to your accuser, "The Lord rebuke you!" for you will be clothed in perfect white. Paul asks, "Who is he that condemns? Christ Jesus, who died—more than that, who was raised to life—is at the right hand of God and is also interceding for us" (Rom. 8:34).

Darkness and Light

However, not everyone in this encounter went away forgiven. Not everyone today stands uncondemned before God. Jesus put it this way: "For God so loved the world that he gave his one and only Son, that whoever believes in him shall not perish but have eternal life . . . but whoever does not believe stands condemned already because he has not believed in the name of God's one and only Son" (John 3:16, 18).

The scribes and Pharisees, so sure of their moral stature because of their outward religion and petty works, departed condemned because they rejected the Son of God and Savior. If they represent you, your reliance on your works, your contempt for those in sin and disgrace, then learn that Christ will send you away, only to stand before God's throne in the day of judgment. And you will hear the verdict, "All have sinned, and fall short of the glory of God" (Rom. 3:23).

Then there was the crowd, interested in the passing excitement but blind to the realities at hand. They witnessed forgiveness but did nothing to gain it for themselves; they were curious, indifferent, and uninvolved. If you are like them, then beware, for you will not remain uninvolved but will be called to answer for your sins.

Then there was this woman. Perhaps you feel like her. Disgraced by your sin. Wearied by guilt. Your blood running cold with fear, hell itself staring into your face as you contemplate God's judgment. Then look upon this Christ, look upon your Savior. He says to you, if you look to him in faith, "Neither do I condemn you. Go now and leave your life of sin." As Martin Luther well put it: "If you have tasted the Law and sin, and if you know the ache of sin, then look here, and see how sweet, in comparison, the grace of God is, the grace which is offered to us in the Gospel."[7] And seeing that grace, you will not want to sin any longer but will seek grace from Christ to walk in newness of life.

"I am the light of the world," Jesus said, when next he addressed the crowd. "Whoever follows me will never walk in darkness, but will have the light of life" (John 8:12). If you will look out of your darkness and into the light of his grace, so shall it be for you.

5

Jesus and the Fisherman

Luke 5:1–11

When he had finished speaking, he said to Simon, "Put out into deep water, and let down the nets for a catch." Simon answered, "Master, we've worked hard all night and haven't caught anything. But because you say so, I will let down the nets." (Luke 5:4–5)

So far, the encounters with Jesus we have examined have been from the Gospel of John. Those meetings, featuring a scholar and statesman, two sinful women, and a disabled man, served as vehicles to present to us the marvelous grace that is in Christ. This is in keeping with John's summary, "The law was given through Moses; grace and truth came through Jesus Christ" (John 1:17).

Beginning with this passage in Luke 5, we turn to the Synoptic Gospels to see more encounters with Jesus. These Gospels—Matthew, Mark, and Luke—called Synoptic because of their basic similarity—present a somewhat different emphasis. To encounter Jesus is always to encounter grace, but here there is also a strong challenge to follow him, a costly discipleship that cannot be avoided.

In 1937, a young German theologian named Dietrich Bonhoeffer published his famous book, *The Cost of Discipleship*. He began by pointing out that the biblical description of the Christian life is that of discipleship. Christians are followers of Jesus and bearers of his cross. Bonhoeffer was motivated in writing by a concern for what he called "cheap grace." Grace, he observed, is freely given by God, and yet it costs the believer everything. He wrote,

> Cheap grace is the preaching of forgiveness without requiring repentance, baptism without church discipline, absolution without personal confession. Cheap grace is grace without discipleship, grace without the cross, grace without Jesus Christ, living and incarnate.[1]

Bonhoeffer got the chance to live out his convictions. He was teaching theology at Berlin University when Adolf Hitler came to power in 1933. Bonhoeffer went on German radio and denounced the idolatry of the Hitler cult. After six months of struggle against the Nazis, he escaped to London. In 1935, however, he returned to organize an underground seminary for the confessing movement of German churches. During the world war that followed, Bonhoeffer was arrested by the Nazis, and a few days before the war's end he was cruelly put to death.

Dietrich Bonhoeffer did not believe in salvation without discipleship to Jesus Christ, without following him and bearing his cross in the world. He reminded us that Jesus taught, "If anyone would come after me, he must deny himself and take up his cross daily and follow me" (Luke 9:23). But Bonhoeffer did not find the cross just at the end of his life's journey. As he wrote, "The cross is not the terrible end to an otherwise god-fearing and happy life, but it meets us at the beginning of our communion with Christ."[2] It is the cross, a dying to this world and to sin, that defines the whole of the Christian life of discipleship.

If that is true, and it is, then it was a reality Simon the son of John had been trying to avoid. The encounter described in Luke 5 was not his first meeting with Jesus. His brother Andrew had been with John the Baptist when the prophet saw and identified Jesus, saying, "Look, the Lamb of God!" (John 1:36). Andrew immediately found his brother, told him, "We have found the Messiah" (John 1:41), and brought him to meet Jesus. On the third day after this, Jesus went with his disciples to the wedding at Cana, so it is nearly certain that Simon witnessed the first miracle of Jesus' public ministry there.

It is clear in Luke's Gospel that Jesus and Simon had an ongoing relationship of sorts, because in Luke 4:38–39 Jesus went to Simon's home and healed his mother-in-law from a dangerous fever. Simon therefore had met Jesus, he was part of the circle of his disciples, and Simon had not yet committed himself to Jesus.

Our passage in this chapter presents the decisive encounter that resulted in Simon committing himself as a true disciple of Jesus. At the beginning of the passage he is still going about his work, still living the life he had before. He was like so many today who know about Jesus, who have seen some of the reality of his power, who even have identified him as a transcendent figure. But they have yet to make the decisive commitment; they have yet to follow Jesus Christ as his disciple. By the end of this encounter everything will have changed for Simon, known to us as the apostle Peter. What Bonhoeffer describes as the true encounter with Christ will have happened to him: "It is the dying of the old man which is the result of his encounter with Christ."[3]

I want to consider three actions on the part of Jesus that produced this transformation: first, a lesson in faith, second, an application of grace, and third, a compelling call that could not be denied.

A Lesson in Faith

Jesus was at the Lake of Gennesaret teaching a great crowd of people. This event takes place early in his ministry, during the Galilean phase when our Lord was healing multitudes and drawing great crowds. Along the water's edge he found two boats conveniently left empty, and Jesus got into one. It happened to be owned and captained by Simon the son of John, whom Jesus had already gotten to know. Jesus asked Simon to take him a bit away from the shore, and while Simon managed the boat Jesus sat down and began preaching. Simon probably had heard the message about God's kingdom already, but it is apparent that it had not sunk in. We think of Jesus' later parable of the soils, and it is not difficult to conclude that Simon's faith was like the seed that fell among the thorns, representing the cares of this world, which choked the seed to keep it from growing.

We are not told of any effect Jesus' teaching had on Simon. I wouldn't be surprised if he was barely listening, thinking mainly about the hard night before on the lake and the empty nets he and the other fishermen brought back to the shore. But, as we have seen before, Jesus asked a service of the one he intended to save and employ. If Simon was daydreaming, his attention was grasped when Jesus finished his sermon, turned to him, and said, "Put out into deep water, and let down the nets for a catch" (Luke 5:4).

This was the beginning of the lesson of faith Jesus was going to teach. Simon was a fisherman; indeed, he was the captain of his boat and little business enterprise. Jesus was a preacher and a former carpenter. Therefore this command is extraordinary, and we see some of Simon's reluctance to follow the unsolicited advice.

Simon answered Jesus, "Master, we've worked hard all night and haven't caught anything." I don't think we have to read too deeply between the lines to pick up on Simon's attitude. "These preachers think that because they know a little Bible, they know everything! If we haven't caught any fish here in the dark, then anybody with experience knows we won't catch any here in the bright daylight." But, perhaps because of his respect for Jesus as the rising rabbi, or master, as Peter calls him, perhaps out of deference for the man who had healed his mother-in-law, Simon consented. "Because you say so, I will let down the nets." The reluctance of his obedience is evident. How stunned, then, Simon was at the result! "They caught such a large number of fish that their nets began to break. So they signaled their partners in the other boat to come and help them, and they came and filled both boats so full that they began to sink" (Luke 5:6–7).

This result made clear the lesson Jesus was trying to convey: his word is to be trusted and obeyed. It is a lesson about faith because it is a lesson about Jesus. Jesus was disclosing his divine nature. This miracle shows his supernatural knowledge—the kind that could know the exact location of the fish beneath the water's surface—and it shows his power as well, for as Simon immediately recognized, this was neither luck nor skill but a display of divine power over the created realm. With this display, Jesus tellingly revealed that he is competent to guide those who are with him, able to provide, and therefore worthy of their trust.

This is something Christians need to learn about our Lord as well. Often we receive a duty or obligation from the Lord in Scripture and we think that obeying will be unprofitable for us. We think we will lose out on the things other people are gaining; we will fail to have our wants and our needs provided for. But when we follow at Christ's command, because it is he who leads us, we find a supernatural abundance in the most unexpected of places.

Think, for instance, of our duties in marriage. Women are commanded to respect and submit to their husbands. This sounds unwise and ill judged. "What does Jesus know about being a wife to my husband," a woman says, much the way Simon objected to Jesus' fishing advice. "If I obey Jesus' word I will be taken advantage of; I will lose out." The truth, however, is that if she will obey Jesus, she will find a sweetness and joy she could not have known without the duty Christ gave to her. Christ blesses what he commands, making all our duties sweet and filling our nets with abundance.

The same is true for husbands, who are given the duty of putting their wives' interest above their own, as Christ loved the church by dying for her. This seems dreary to men, to give up things in which they have an interest just to be with her, to sacrifice free time and leisure energy ministering to her temporal and spiritual needs. But when

Christians perform their given duties by faith, Christ fills the net with spiritual blessing, and very often temporal blessing as well. Faithful husbands are repaid with an intimacy and satisfaction that cannot be had without the duty. Christ's grace makes the duty a joy.

I cite the example of marriage illustratively. The same applies in difficult work settings, where Christians have the duty of respecting their boss; in families, where we must honor our parents; in the church, where we respect authority and serve humbly and sacrificially. These things are our duty. But we are wrong to think that Christ commands them to our detriment. Instead he goes with us to ensure the blessing of an abundance only he can provide.

Jesus demonstrated to Simon on his terms, by means of this filling of the nets, why he is to be trusted and obeyed. Simon was reluctant at first, but he acted with a brief phrase upon his lips, and that was the key to blessing. He said: "Because you say so," or, as an older version puts it, "At thy word." Charles Spurgeon picks up on this, writing:

> "At thy word" has been the password of all good men from the beginning until now. . . . An ark is builded on dry land, and the ribald crowd gather about the hoary patriarch, laughing at him; but he is not ashamed, for lifting his face to heaven he saith, "I have builded this great vessel, O Jehovah, at thy word." Abraham quits the place of his childhood, leaves his family and goes with Sarah to a land of which he knows nothing. . . . He dwells in tents with Isaac and Jacob. If any scoff at him for thus renouncing his comforts of settled life he lifts also his calm face to heaven and smilingly answers to the Lord, "It is at thy word." . . . Moses lifts his

rod in the presence of haughty Pharaoh, "at thy word," great God! Nor does he lift that rod in vain at Jehovah's word, for thick and heavy fall the plagues upon the children of Ham.

It was into this great roll call of faith that Jesus was initiating Simon Peter; and into it we too are called by the testimony of the Bible. Spurgeon concludes:

> This ought to be the rule of all Christians for the whole of their lives, "At thy word." This should direct us in the church and in the world; it should guide us in our spiritual beliefs and in our secular acts. "At thy word." . . . The power of the church and the power of the individual to please God shall never be fully known until we get back to the simple yet sublime rule of our text, "At thy word."[4]

An Application of Grace

That was the lesson of faith Jesus taught to Simon Peter, a primer based on his ability to lead and provide. Simon got the point, which he had never grasped before. When it was in his professional arena, in terms Simon most clearly understood, the scales fell that had previously clouded his eyes. Such is Christ's sensitivity to individuals, his willingness to meet us where we are in order to gain our trust. Indeed, this miracle opened Simon's eyes wide to a greater spiritual reality. Seeing this great harvest of fish, one that could not be accounted for by any but divine power, for once Simon Peter connected the dots in rapid succession and comprehended the enormity of what was before his eyes. Luke tells us, "When Simon Peter saw this, he fell at

Jesus' knees and said, 'Go away from me, Lord; I am a sin-ful man!' For he and all his companions were astonished at the catch of fish they had taken, and so were James and John, the sons of Zebedee, Simon's partners" (Luke 5:8–10).

Luke 5:7 tells us their boat was overloaded with fish and beginning to sink. But with his flash of insight regarding the person of Jesus, Peter thought nothing of his great phys-ical danger but only of his great spiritual danger, the peril of his soul: "He fell at Jesus' knees and said, 'Go away from me, Lord; I am a sinful man!'"

How are we to account for this remarkable response? A psychologist would no doubt say it had something to do with childhood inadequacies that were brought to the sur-face. Or perhaps Peter was somewhat unbalanced, prone to anxiety and fear, uneasy and paranoid because of a moralis-tic upbringing. This is the kind of analysis modern scholars have applied to Martin Luther, the great Reformer. Luther's idiosyncrasies were legion, but most noteworthy were his deep awareness of sin and absolute dread of the holy. An in-cident from his initiation as a priest is perhaps the most telling indicator about his state of mind. After several years as a monk, Luther was to celebrate his first mass as a priest. But when he stepped up to the altar and prepared to speak the vital words that supposedly would turn the bread and wine into the body and blood of Christ, Luther froze solid. Years later he explained:

> I was utterly stupefied and terror-stricken. I thought to myself, "With what tongue shall I address such majesty, seeing that all men ought to tremble in the presence of even an earthly prince? Who am I, that I should lift up mine eyes or raise my hands to the

divine Majesty? The angels surround him. At his nod the earth trembles. And shall I, a miserable little pygmy, say, 'I want this, I ask for that'? For I am dust and ashes and full of sin and I am speaking to the living, eternal and the true God."[5]

In his presentation of this story, R. C. Sproul allows that maybe Luther was a little crazy. "But," he adds, "if he was, our prayer is that God would send to this earth an epidemic of such insanity."[6] What drove Luther and Simon Peter crazy, what drove them to their knees, was a glimpse of the holiness of God, an awareness that they were standing before the divine presence, and a terrifying comprehension of their sin.

The great biblical example of this is found in Isaiah 6, when the young Isaiah went into the temple and was confronted by a theophany, that is, a manifestation of the presence of God.

> I saw the Lord seated on a throne, high and exalted, and the train of his robe filled the temple. Above him were seraphs, each with six wings. . . . And they were calling out to one another:
> "Holy, holy, holy is the LORD Almighty;
> the whole earth is full of his glory."
> (Isa. 6:1–3)

Isaiah's response to that vision was the same as Peter's, the same as Luther's. "'Woe to me!' I cried. 'I am ruined! For I am a man of unclean lips, and I live among a people of unclean lips, and my eyes have seen the King, the LORD Almighty'" (v. 5). Like Peter in the boat with Jesus, whom he now saw as divine, Isaiah was most uncomfortable. It is the kind of discomfort thieves have in the presence of policemen. But of course, it is far worse than that. These men who comprehended the reality of God and knew themselves as sinners were "undone," "ruined." Sproul says of Isaiah, and it can apply equally to Peter:

> He caught one sudden glimpse of a Holy God. In that single moment all of his self-esteem was shattered. In a brief second he was exposed, made naked beneath the gaze of the absolute standard of holiness. . . . The instant he measured himself by the ultimate standard, he was destroyed—morally and spiritually annihilated. He was undone.[7]

You compare this with the easy, breezy spirituality of our time, and you see quite a contrast. To so many today, Jesus is a good dude, a buddy and a pal. We treat him not with reverence and awe but with flippant familiarity, the kind that breeds contempt. It is true that Jesus is a friend to sinners because of the nature of his saving work. But we must realize as Christians that we are confronted with a holy God in Jesus Christ. It was the exalted Jesus Isaiah saw in his temple vision, as John 12:41 tells us. Therefore true spirituality is characterized not by joviality and lighthearted fun, much less by carnal enthusiasm, but is built upon dread of God's holiness and loathing for our sin.

That is hardly, you may note, the kind of spirituality that draws people close to the Lord. It didn't draw Peter close. "Depart from me, Lord," he cried, and that is not the highest expression of spiritual communion with Christ. Perhaps not, but it is the proper and necessary precursor. God says in Isaiah,

> I live in a high and holy place,
>> but also with him who is contrite and lowly in
>>> spirit,
>> to revive the spirit of the lowly
>> and to revive the heart of the contrite.
>> (Isa. 57:15)

If you have not stood in anguish for sin before the holiness of God, there to receive the grace of Christ, then perhaps it is because you, like Peter before this encounter, have only been toying with Jesus Christ. You have been an acquaintance, yes, but not a disciple, not a recipient of the grace he gives only to brokenhearted sinners.

The terror of the holy, the dread of punishment for sin, is the precursor for the true receipt of the gospel. For Luther, his dread of condemnation opened his eyes to the doctrine of justification by faith alone, the biblical teaching that our sins are forgiven by faith in the cross of Christ. For Isaiah, his self-rejection was the proper start for a life of being God's herald of salvation in Israel. As Isaiah stood in the temple in abject repentance, not merely of his sins but of himself, he tells us, "One of the seraphs flew to me with a live coal in his hand, which he had taken with tongs from the altar. With it he touched my mouth and said, 'See, this has touched your lips; your guilt is taken away and your sin atoned for'" (Isa. 6:6–7). The coal came from the altar on which the sacrifices were offered; Isaiah was cleansed by the blood of the lamb, his prophetic lips consecrated with an ember from that offering fire.

We find this same grace for Simon Peter, undone as he was with dread for his sin. Jesus said to him, "Don't be afraid" (Luke 5:10). "Fear not," he said, and that was the application of his grace to the holy terror that had seized the future apostle. We are intentionally reminded of what the angel said to Mary, at the annunciation of Christ's birth. "Do not be afraid, Mary, you have found favor with God" (Luke 1:30). So also with Peter; he had found favor, that is, grace from the Lord. Mary was going to give birth to the only Son of God; Peter was going to become a fisher of men.

"Fear not," God says to every contrite sinner, undone with an awareness of sin and of God's holiness, who comes to him through faith in Jesus Christ. There is no fear because there is now no condemnation for those Christ calls by his grace, because he lays down his life for his sheep. "I give them eternal life," Jesus says of those who hear and follow, "and they shall never perish; no one can snatch them out of my hand" (John 10:28). Therefore, he says to you, rightly afraid to draw near to God, "Fear not. Do not be afraid." The lesson in faith, when received, always leads to an application of grace.

A Compelling Call

That application of grace is always followed by a call to discipleship. Where there is the grace of Christ there is also this call, the call to follow Jesus and serve his kingdom.

Grace removes every obstacle to such service. Sin is no longer a barrier, for Christ deals with our sin. Neither is weakness a barrier, because his grace supplies the power. Peter had not even been that great a fisher of fish—now he is to be a fisher of men! How? Because of the promise and power of Christ, as demonstrated by the miraculous catch that overwhelmed Peter's boat. It is on the basis of these—his promise and his power—that every Christian follows Christ.

Jesus called Peter into his service with a promise: "From now on you will catch men." He did not simply give a command, "Go out and start fishing for men." No, the calling went with a promise, a promised founded on Christ's transforming power. In the versions of Matthew and Mark this is perhaps clearer. Jesus said to Peter and his friends, "Come, follow me, and I will make you fishers of men" (Mark 1:17). What Christ demands from us, he produces in us and makes of us.

Peter and his friends are not the only ones called to follow Jesus. The calling is to all who have encountered Jesus, received his grace and with it the invitation into the work of the ages, the harvest of souls as fellow workers of the Lord. It was with such a charge that Jesus departed from this earth, as told to us in the parting lines of Matthew's Gospel: "Go and make disciples of all nations, baptizing them in the name of the Father and of the Son and of the Holy Spirit, and teaching them to obey everything I have commanded you" (Matt. 28:19–20).

That is a charge we lack the power to accomplish, as Peter must have realized from the start. No doubt that is why he stayed close to Jesus, because the promise he adds makes all the difference. Jesus assured us, "Surely I am with you always, to the very end of the age" (Matt. 28:20). Therefore we are to be with him always, abiding in him, following where he leads, for his is the power the calling demands.

The Cost of Discipleship

Let me conclude by making two points. The first comes from Jesus' promise to Peter, "From now on you will catch men." If you have personally encountered Jesus, if you have learned from him faith, received from him grace, then there has been that kind of definitive break in your life as well. You understand, if you are a Christian, the meaning of the words "from now on." A true and personal encounter with the Lord Jesus Christ always bears this stamp. There is a before coming to Jesus. And there is a from now on. As Luther wrote about this passage, no doubt with reflection on his experience, "Peter is to become a different man; and a greater miracle is to be wrought in him than in the draught of fishes."[8] So it is for all who are called to follow Jesus.

Second, we see that the mark of this definitive break, this life-changing call, is the one we find in Luke 5:11, "So they pulled their boats up on shore, left everything and followed him." Bonhoeffer spoke of this as the cost of discipleship. He wrote, "When Christ calls a man, he bids him come and die."[9] For him that meant leaving the safety of silence to speak against Hitler and ultimately the loss of his life in a Gestapo detention camp. Luther left the monastery and its protection, standing up against the Roman Catholic Church to be a preacher of grace through faith in Christ. Isaiah left the temple changed forever, no longer a prominent citizen but a prophet of the thrice-holy God. Simon Peter and his friends left their fishing boats to follow Jesus. They left to be fishers of men, staying close to Jesus, who gives the promise and the power needed for such a task.

I don't know exactly what it means for you to follow Jesus. But I do know this: If you come to him as a sinner seeking grace, you will not be turned away by him. He came to be the Savior of sinners. And I know this, too, that if you have heard the words from Jesus, "Fear not!" then he has called you to follow him as a disciple. To follow him, you will have to die to your former way of life, one way or another. You will have to leave things behind—your love of sin and your worldly outlook, but perhaps also relationships, prior goals and dreams you had before encountering him, habits and ambitions, perhaps like Peter even your occupation.

Finally, I know this as well. If you leave all to follow Jesus, you will not be sorry in the end. You will not lose out. Your nets will not be empty in the waters to which he has called you. You will know, through faith in him, an abundance of life that only he can give. As Jesus taught, "For whoever wants to save his life will lose it, but whoever loses his life for me will save it" (Luke 9:24).

6

Jesus and the Tax Collector

Matthew 9:9–13

As Jesus went on from there, he saw a man named Matthew sitting at the tax collector's booth. "Follow me," he told him, and Matthew got up and followed him. (Matt. 9:9)

The best stories tell a rags-to-riches tale. In politics you have Abraham Lincoln, who rose from the log cabin to the White House. In business, we admire those like Sam Walton, who by hard work, smarts, and sheer pluck, drove his pick-up truck all the way to general-store billions. In sports we love the guy who began the season as a supermarket clerk and ended it as the winning quarterback in the Super Bowl. These are the stories that fire our imagination, that speak of hope for all the rest of us. These are the kind of tales immortalized in the movies: *Mr. Smith Goes to Washington*, *My Fair Lady*, and perhaps the greatest sports movie of all time, *Rocky*. The name most strongly associated with such stories is Horatio Alger, who made himself famous over a century ago with novel after novel extolling success through the virtues of honesty, hard work, self-reliance, and perseverance.

When it comes to rags-to-riches stories, the Bible is not to be outdone. Indeed, the Bible is the greatest teller of shocking but true accounts of triumph and dramatic turnarounds. Here we find the shepherd boy David, slaying giant Goliath with a stone and rising to become Israel's greatest king. Here we find the Pharisee Saul, the great persecutor of the early church, transformed into the apostle Paul, its greatest preacher of grace. And then there is the account in Matthew 9, the calling of Matthew the tax collector to become a disciple and later an apostle of the Lord Jesus Christ. None of these, however, are tales of human achievement but rather of divine grace, which is the Bible's theme. As John Calvin writes about our passage: "That Matthew from his tax office should have been received into Christ's fellowship, yes, and called to the office of an Apostle, is an illustrious example for us of the grace of God."[1]

Matthew the Tax Collector

The Bible approves of Alger's ideals of individual initiative, honesty, hard work, and perseverance. But this account before us is not about these. It was not Matthew's initiative that led to his salvation. He was not looking for Jesus, was not hoping for a change, was not trying to get out of his sinful condition. In this respect he was just like the rest of us.

Paul writes in Romans 3:10–11, "There is no one right-eous, not even one . . . no one who seeks God." Man in his sin has initiative when it comes to things like promotion, riches, and fame. But man is not interested in the things of God. What sinful man wants is sin, either openly or dis-creetly. Self-serving man wants self-glory and self-indulgence. Since the knowledge of God leads away from these things, man is neither willing nor able to seek God. By nature we are opposed to the things of God, and therefore no initia-tive of ours is ever going to lead to salvation.

Matthew the tax collector is a prime example of the human condition. Our text tells us that Jesus was walking along and saw Matthew "sitting at the tax collector's booth." In the context of this time there could hardly be a more fitting symbol of godlessness than the tax collector. In the Roman Empire, bids were taken for the right to collect taxes in a given region. Those who won them were required to pay a set amount to Rome, but anything they collected above that amount they could keep. You can see where this led. The tax collectors preyed upon the people and espe-cially those who practiced trade, all for the sake of their own enrichment.

In Judea this was made worse by the fact that the tax collectors were collaborating with the occupying enemy. Their business and associations left them in a perpetual state of ceremonial uncleanness. According to the Jewish writings of the time, if a tax gatherer even set foot in your house, every object and person within was rendered un-clean (*Toharot* 7:6). These were people who spurned na-tional and family loyalties, who cared nothing for spiritual or religious matters. They are rightly compared with the drug pushers of today, rich in money but despicable by every other standard.

That is what tax collectors were like, and as such they are a particularly glaring example of what is true of us all, apart from Christ. Like Matthew at his booth, we are immersed in a way of life opposed to God. He was sitting there at the tax collector's booth as Jesus came by, no doubt content with his state and with no intention of being moved from his pattern of life. Paul says the same of us all, apart from Christ: "They are darkened in their understanding and separated from the life of God because of the ignorance that is in them due to the hardening of their hearts" (Eph. 4:18). That is the way of all mankind, seated and determined in godlessness.

The Calling of Matthew

Yet, despite Matthew's self-satisfied and darkened condition, Jesus came to call this tax collector to be his disciple. Matthew 9:9 tells us that Jesus "saw a man named Matthew sitting at the tax collector's booth. 'Follow me,' he told him." This account provides us with an excellent opportunity to reflect biblically on an important theological theme, namely, the call of Christ. In particular, we see the difference between the general or outward call of the gospel and the effectual and inward call that produces salvation.

Matthew's tax station would have been in an extremely public place. The commentators place it at either the docks along the lake, to collect taxes from the shipbound trade, or along the main road leading into town. In either case, Matthew would have listened to Jesus' teaching or have heard much about it from those who passed by. The events of Matthew 9:1–8, the healing of the paralytic, had just taken place in Capernaum, Matthew's home. Mark's account tells us there had been so many people crowded around the house in which Jesus was teaching that the paralytic's friends had to let him down through a hole they made in the roof. You could not have been in this town without being a party in one way or another to astonishing events like that. Therefore we can be certain that Matthew had heard of Jesus' preaching and knew of his miraculous works.

Nonetheless there is no evidence that this had the slightest impact on Matthew the tax collector. There he was in his booth, carrying on his business without any discernible response to all these affairs. In this he offers an outstanding example of what we call the general call of the gospel. Jesus taught openly before all the people, just as today the gospel is preached before the crowds. "Come to me," Jesus calls, and all are free to come and be saved. The call goes forth in earnest; it is a true invitation. But it is not effectual. It is universal in its outreach, genuine in its offer. But it is not accepted by the mass of people who, like Matthew at his booth, are not interested in salvation or in Jesus Christ. If Matthew derived any lesson from what he heard, it must have been that whatever was being offered had no relevance to him; he was too far gone to consider talk of repentance and faith.

It was not the general call that saved Matthew but the particular, the inward, the effectual call of Jesus Christ to salvation. Matthew 9:9 puts it bluntly: " 'Follow me,' Jesus said, "and Matthew got up and followed him." The brevity of this account emphasizes the radical character of what took place. Jesus described this same phenomenon in John 10:3, when he says of himself as the Good Shepherd: "The sheep listen to his voice. He calls his own sheep by name and leads them out." Christ's effectual call is personal, and it is mighty.

This is the voice that called Lazarus from the grave, that stilled the storm upon the lake, that silenced and subdued the demons. Christ's call is different from every other call. His personal call is effectual because it goes forth with his power to save. It is the same power that healed the paralytic, when he said, "Get up! Pick up your mat and walk" (John 5:8). His is the very voice of God, the voice that said, " 'Let there be light,' and there was light" (Gen. 1:3). Therefore, when Jesus sent forth his effectual call, saying to Matthew, "Come, follow me," Matthew came, got up from his sin, and was saved.

Effectual calling is related to the great Calvinistic doctrine of irresistible grace. Irresistible grace does not mean that God's grace is never resisted by human beings. We see evidence that it is every day. What the doctrine means is that conversion is the result of a grace that is irresistible. It means that when Christ through the Holy Spirit adds his effectual and saving call to the general call of the gospel, that person he calls comes. Charles Spurgeon compares it with the summons of an English monarch:

> When the Queen sends to anybody to come and see her, she does not "request the pleasure of his company," but she sends her command to him to come. That is the way kings and queens talk; and that is just the way with the Lord Jesus Christ, the King of kings, and Lord of lords. He says, "Follow me." . . . and with that command goes the power of the word of a King, and so sinners are saved.[2]

People object to this teaching, saying that God cannot do violence to our free will. The answer to that complaint is that God can, although "violence" poorly describes the sweet and regenerating work of his grace. If God does not interfere with our natural course, if he does not enter in and impose his gracious will, then none ever will be saved. It is true that God does not work his grace so as to coerce our will, so that we respond in an unwilling manner. Quite the contrary! He changes our will as the potter molds the clay. He changes our affections and beliefs and attitudes so that we respond out of new hearts with eager faith and are saved with joyful tears.

The fact is that our wills are not free. When we speak of the will, we are describing our decision making, our faculty of volition, something that certainly is very real. But the will is not free; it is determined by our thoughts and desires. We choose what we think is best, what we want. This is why Jesus said in John 8:34, "I tell you the truth, everyone who sins is a slave to sin." We sin because it is our nature to love sin; we are sinners. So much for free will! The will, under the power of sin, is captive and bound. Augustine rightly pointed out so many years ago: "Free will without grace has the power to do nothing but sin."[3]

You see why the effectual call of Christ is such good news, because it teaches that God saves and converts his own with an irresistible grace. It was God's promise of this good news that Ezekiel spoke of: "I will give you a new heart and put a new spirit in you; I will remove from you your heart of stone and give you a heart of flesh. And I will put my Spirit in you and move you to follow my decrees and be careful to keep my laws" (Ezek. 36:26–27). That is what God does in the effectual call, and this is the explanation for what happens in conversion. People tell us to give our heart to Jesus, but God does not want such a filthy thing as that. Instead he has a new heart to give to us, and with that new heart we then give the whole of ourselves, trusting and loving and eagerly serving the One who has loved us so well.

Implications of the Doctrine

Let me work out some of the relevant implications of this, the first of which has to do with assurance of salvation. This teaching gives us the answer to the important question Why are some saved while others are not? People answer, "Because some believe and others don't." All right, then why do some believe whereas others do not? The answer is that God sovereignly chose some for salvation; by grace alone he chose to save those sinners who believe. As Acts 13:48 shows, it is those "who were appointed for eternal life" who believe. Therefore, if you have believed, it is because in the midst of the general call going out through your city, your campus, your church, God's effectual call came to you with his irresistible grace. As John Wesley said of his conversion, "My heart was strangely warmed." The salvation of rebellious, hard-hearted sinners *is* strange, so strange that the only explanation is God's sovereign, intervening grace. So it was for Matthew the tax collector turned disciple of Christ. So it is for everyone called from darkness into light, from unbelief into faith.

This is great good news. For if your coming to faith rested upon your will, then remaining in faith also depends on your will. You, then, are at the mercy of your human will in days ahead, and upon it rests your eternal destiny. That is not good news for sinners. But if it was the sovereign, saving work of the almighty God in which you were saved then you may rest assured, as Paul wrote in Philippians 1:6, "that he who began a good work in you will carry it on to completion until the day of Christ Jesus."

The doctrine of the effectual call gives us, first, confidence about our salvation, because it tells us that salvation ultimately depends upon God and not upon us (Rom. 9:16). But, second, the doctrine of effectual calling inspires confidence for our witness to others. I assure you that this teaching makes all the difference to a preacher of the gospel. If preachers have to rely upon their powers to get sinners to love God, to make believers out of unbelievers, to gain worship for God out of idolaters, then they rightly tremble to ever venture into a pulpit. A rejection of this doctrine would influence a minister's style of preaching, and when doctrines like effectual calling are denied, it does! No longer do preachers feel free to simply set forth the Word of God. Instead they must to resort to trickery, to manipulation, to subtle artifice. This great doctrine makes all the difference to a preacher, and in the same way it makes all the difference to your Christian witness. It was because of his belief that salvation is God's work that Paul could say of his ministry, "We do not use deception, nor do we distort the word of God. On the contrary, by setting forth the truth plainly we commend ourselves to every man's conscience in the sight of God" (2 Cor. 4:2).

It is not the preacher's business to convert sinners but rather to preach Christ's gospel. We sound the general call, with all the gifts and energy we have, but Christ sends forth his Spirit to make it effectual to his own. Likewise, it is not a Christian's work to regenerate his family member, neighbor, or friend. Yours is to bear testimony with confidence, knowing that God is pleased to convert the lost by his power and to the glory of his name.

That leads to the third implication of this doctrine, that since salvation is by grace, by God's effectual power that goes forth with the gospel, then all the glory belongs to him alone. Matthew's salvation was of sovereign grace to the glory of God. Nothing indicates any merit on Matthew's part. He was not praying when Christ came to him. He was not reading his Bible. He was not doing good works. Indeed, it was quite the opposite. What we have here is what Paul described as the rule for us all, in Titus 3:3–5: "We too were foolish, disobedient, deceived and enslaved by all kinds of passions and pleasures. We lived in malice and envy, being hated and hating one another. But when the kindness and love of God our Savior appeared, he saved us, not because of righteous things we had done, but because of his mercy." Thus Matthew's conversion, like every other conversion, proves again the great statement of Jonah 2:9, "Salvation comes from the LORD."

The last implication I want to point out is that because of this great teaching, Christians have no right to despair of anyone's salvation. God can make an apostle out of a tax collector. John Newton once remarked, "Since God saved me I despair of no man's salvation," and likewise we must withhold the gospel from none, knowing that through the gospel Christ has effectual power to save anyone.

Matthew's Witness to Others

There is a wealth of theology displayed in Matthew 9:9 alone. Jesus said, "'Follow me,' and Matthew got up and followed him." For Matthew, this was not merely a theological matter but a personal one. We have to remember that the author of this account was also its subject. We can well imagine the tears that welled up in Matthew's eyes as he lifted his pen to this portion of his Gospel. If we could see the original manuscript, I can imagine we would find small smudges on the page where teardrops fell. His thoughts would have returned to an oh-so-distant time and place, with renewed wonder and thanksgiving. "Jesus saw me," he writes. "He spoke. And I arose." That is the testimony of every sinner ever saved.

I have noted that this account comes hard upon the healing of the paralytic. All three Synoptic Gospels place it here, so the chronology is quite certain. But surely there is a thematic connection as well. We see the miracle of the paralytic who is healed and rises to his feet. Along with it is this marvel of grace, perhaps an even greater display of saving power, as the tax collector rises from his sin and follows Jesus.

Whenever we consider the miracles of Christ, we should think of our salvation. The blind man sees—yes, I was blind, but now I see. The demon-possessed is delivered—ah, I was bound by Satan and by sin, and Christ set free my heart. The lame man gets up and walks—yes, I was sitting in my weakness and my sin. Christ called me, and so I walked with him into life eternal. Our teardrops too should wet the pages of the Gospel text. Our experiences are not all the same, and not all of us will have a dramatic conversion experience like Matthew's, but all Christians can give this testimony: "I was caught in sin, powerless to arise, unwilling and unable to follow the ways of God. But Jesus set his eyes on me, he spoke to my heart, and now I am his by God's saving grace."

But Matthew's conversion story does not stop there. Our passage goes on to give abundant testimony that Matthew had started a new life. Matthew 9:10 speaks of a dinner he held in his house, probably that very day. He brought Jesus and the other disciples, along with "many tax collectors and 'sinners.' " If there is any one sign of new life in Christ, this is it—the fervent desire for others to meet Jesus and also be saved. Paul writes, "I believed; therefore I have spoken" (2 Cor. 4:13), and so must it be for us all.

Every Christian must be a witness for Christ. And yet we find in the Bible an amazing variety of testimonies. There is a great difference between Nicodemus and the woman at the well, but both of them would publicly express their faith in their own way. In our last study we saw the calling of Simon Peter as a fisher of men. Now we have Matthew the tax collector, whose conversion drew all sorts of other sinners to Jesus, with many, no doubt, saved as a result. Far from having only one approach, Jesus employs his people with an amazing degree of variety. He called Peter to be a fisherman; Matthew he called to be bait.

Matthew's evangelistic approach is an especially noteworthy example for us. First, he opened up his home and reached out to people he already knew. Second, he introduced sinners to Jesus Christ and Jesus Christ to sinners, and that is what evangelism is all about.

We can imagine the scene there well enough. Matthew would have said to one of his sinful friends, "I want you to meet Jesus," and to Jesus he would have said, "Master, here is a friend of mine." That is how evangelism takes place. The role of our testimony is to introduce people to Jesus, to tell who he is and what he has done. Just as Matthew invited these sinners to his house, we invite people to our homes and to the church to learn about the Savior. In prayer we do the other side, we introduce Jesus to our unbelieving friends: "Lord, I want to bring to your acquaintance this new neighbor of mine, this old friend, this family member. I commend them to you for your saving grace." That is what evangelism is all about, and it is the work we are all called to do in one way or another.

Christ's Ministry Defended

We have seen an explanation for Matthew's conversion, as well as its manifestation in an evangelistic testimony. Our passage ends with sharp criticism from the ever-watching Pharisees, cowardly addressed not to Jesus but to his disciples: "Why does your teacher eat with tax collectors and 'sinners'?" (Matt. 9:11). In responding to this attack, our Lord defended and defined his ministry while delivering a stinging reproof to these so-called righteous men.

The term *sinners* served a technical function for the Pharisees. They devoted their lives not only to keeping the letter of the law as found in the Bible but also as magnified by the oral traditions of their sect. "Sinners" described not just notorious evildoers but also all of those who did not endorse similar legalistic procedures. This, by its nature, included most of the common people, who had neither the time nor the inclination to lead such an ascetic life. Of central importance to the Pharisees was their refusal to accept table fellowship with anyone who did not follow their code, an attitude Jesus rejected. The Pharisees therefore looked on Jesus' conduct as an affront to them, while also suggesting a cavalier attitude toward the law.

That was the Pharisees' charge against Jesus. His reply served to defend and to define his ministry in the world. First, he responded, "It is not the healthy who need a doctor, but the sick" (Matt. 10:12). Jesus was making two points. First, he noted the Pharisees' attitude of self-righteousness. In their eyes, they were not the sinners but the righteous. Second, he described his ministry as like that of a physician. That being the case, it was no wonder he did not spend his time with those who were well—as the Pharisees considered themselves—but with the sick. Nothing could be more reasonable, and by this means he turned their charge on its head.

It never dawned on the Pharisees that the Messiah might come as a healer for the sick, a redeemer for the lost, a savior for sinners. The very thought was shocking to their minds. They expected him to come as a judge, one who would vindicate them for their outward piety while condemning all their petty enemies. But John 3:17 says, "God did not send his Son into the world to condemn the world, but to save the world through him." Such a thought would appall the Pharisees, who proudly considered themselves beyond the need of salvation. Obviously they had not read or absorbed the teaching of Proverbs 3:34:

> [God] mocks proud mockers
>   but gives grace to the humble.

In Luke 19:10 Jesus tells us why he came: "The Son of Man came to seek and to save what was lost."

You see, then, why Jesus said, "I have not come to call the righteous, but sinners" (Matt. 9:13). It is obvious that he was speaking in irony, pointing out that those who consider themselves righteous disqualify themselves for a ministry like his. That is just as true today. If you are not ready to confess yourself a sinner, then Christ and his gospel are not for you. If you desire not God's mercy but God's justice, then you can try yourself at that bar which says, "Be holy, because I am holy" (Lev. 11:44). The gospel key fits only a door inscribed, "For all have sinned and fall short of the glory of God" (Rom. 3:23). This also means that no one who feels sinful should stay away from this Jesus, but all should come, just as they are, to the Savior of sinners.

To this defense of his ministry Jesus added a stinging reproof. Matthew 9:13 begins with him saying, "But go and learn what this means." That is not a friendly reply to these so-called authorities. Jesus means, "Your remark shows that you are not fit to teach but ought to become disciples and learners." To this he added God's statement in Hosea 6:6, "I desire mercy, not sacrifice."

Jesus is tapping into a whole strain of prophetic teaching, the point of which is that the Old Testament law as a way of salvation hardly expressed the desire of God's heart. This was especially true of the ceremonial portions with the sacrifices and detailed regulations, the things these Pharisees loved. What God wants is not religious ritual but obedience to his will. As sinners, the Pharisees should have come seeking mercy and not a righteousness attained by the slaughter of an occasional animal. Jesus makes clear that if they understood the Scriptures, they would realize that the law expressed not the solution but the problem. The sacrifice of lambs and goats did not remove sin or renew the heart but pointed out the need for a true atonement.

God sent Jesus to be the answer to the problem of sin. God displays his mercy in Christ by gathering sinners to be redeemed by his blood. With that mercy and its results, God is pleased as he never was with the endless sacrifices that did nothing to renew the heart. God is pleased with his mercy extended to sinners in Christ, which achieves a real salvation through the cross and leads to a real change of heart in sinners.

Rags to Riches

In this respect, what the Pharisees abhorred, the idea of the Messiah sitting at table with sinners, is a most glorious portrait of God's love for the world. God is glorified in this, not in the petty displays of the Pharisees. What we have in Matthew 9:10 is a rehearsal for the messianic banquet at the end of the ages, where sinners saved by faith in Christ will sit at the heavenly table in glory.

You see why I refer to this as a great rags-to-riches tale. Every Christian's story is like Matthew's. We begin as sinners and nothing more, and yet Jesus calls us to follow him. I assure you that our company adds little credit to his name in the world, no more than these tax collectors and sinners did. But in the eyes of heaven God is glorified in the highest because of the company he keeps, even sinners redeemed by saving grace, enemies won over by a great redeeming love. That is what Paul says in Ephesians 3:10–11, that God's purpose is that "through the church, the manifold wisdom of God should be made known to the rulers and authorities in the heavenly realms, according to his eternal purpose which he accomplished in Christ Jesus our Lord."

One reason Jesus was happy to be with these sinners, as with us, is that he saw the end from the beginning. Others see the rags; he sees the riches. He saw the crown of righteousness for all who abide in him until the end (2 Tim. 4:8). He knew that everyone he calls will walk with him, learn from him, be molded and shaped by the Spirit of God into his image. And he sees the future, the glorified redeemed, seated on thrones at the banquet feast of the King of kings in heaven.

The greatest such story is the death and resurrection of Jesus Christ, which stands at the center of the Bible's whole message. It is his story that empowers the story of our salvation. It is interesting to observe that the Greek word used to tell us that Matthew stood up when Jesus called him is also the word that describes Jesus rising from the grave. Matthew arose because Jesus would arise, having first put away the tax collector's sins on the cross. The resurrection is the source of Christ's effectual call; it is through the open tomb that the light of a new creation shines to bring about new and saving life in our hearts. Here is the greatest rags-to-riches, dust-to-glory story: the resurrection of the cruci-fied Christ. And most importantly, it is true. It is available to all who trust in him and thus will live with him forever. By all of this God is glorified in the highest for his mercy and power and grace. As Peter remarks in 1 Peter 1:12, "Even angels long to look into these things."

Our story, his glory. That is what the gospel is about. Sinners are saved by the sovereign grace of a merciful God, the spiritually dead arise to newness of life in the hands of the great Physician, outcasts are invited to sit at the banquet of glory forever. "Come, follow me," Jesus says, and if you will, this will be your story, to the praise of his wonderful name.

7

Jesus and the Sinful Woman

Luke 7:36–50

"Therefore, I tell you, her many sins have been forgiven—for she loved much. But he who has been forgiven little loves little." Then Jesus said to her, "Your sins are forgiven." The other guests began to say among themselves, "Who is this who even forgives sins?" (Luke 7:47–49)

Human beings are cognitive simplifiers. That is a fancy term that means we think of things in categories in order to simplify and organize our world. Normally we do this by creating two categories, one that is opposed to the other. We especially do this when it comes to people. "There are two kinds of people," we say. There are the tall and the short, the good-looking and the bad-looking, the smart and

the not-so-smart, minivan versus sport-utility vehicle own-
ers, dog people and cat people.

This way of thinking is reflected in the Bible, perhaps
because it is speaking to the kind of people who think in
terms of two kinds of people. This passage presents exactly
this—two kinds of people. In this encounter from Luke 7
we see several different ways of describing these two kinds
of people. There are those who are convicted by their sense
of sin, and there are those who are not, who consider themselves basically good and righteous. There are those who
love God and those who do not love God. And there are
those who are forgiven their sins and those who are condemned by their sins, which remain upon them.

Biblically there are two kinds of people, and these are
ways they are defined. Those who confess their sin, love
God, and are forgiven are in one group. In the other group
are those who will not confess, do not love God, and are
not forgiven their sins. That is the simple message of this
encounter in Luke 7 between Jesus and the sinful woman in
the house of the Pharisee.

A Striking Encounter

A Pharisee named Simon had invited Jesus to his house for
dinner. There has already been quite a bit of tension between
Jesus and the Pharisees, so this alone is a provocative scene.
No doubt Simon had questions for our Lord, was intending to
assess him up close, to see what all the fuss was about.

Things had not gone far, however, when a disturbance
occurred that was unpleasant for the Pharisee. Luke tells us:

> When a woman who had lived a sinful life in that
> town learned that Jesus was eating at the Pharisee's

house, she brought an alabaster jar of perfume, and as she stood behind him at his feet weeping, she began to wet his feet with her tears. Then she wiped them with her hair, kissed them and poured perfume on them. (Luke 7:37–38)

In these studies of encounters with Jesus, we have been inquiring as to what brought the various people into contact with him. In the case of this Pharisee it is because he was curious at best and malicious at worst. The passage tells us two things about his attitude, namely, that he was assessing the evidence that Jesus might be a prophet and that his hospitality was cold and reluctant. Jesus later criticizes him, saying, "You did not give me any water for my feet. . . . You did not give me a kiss. . . . You did not put oil on my head" (Luke 7:44–46). The Pharisee had not invited Jesus in to worship him or even to fellowship with him warmly but rather to size him up and put him to the test.

The woman, in striking contrast, came because of her fervent love for Jesus Christ. Luke identifies her as a notorious sinner, and the insinuation is that of sexual sin. It is not unlikely that she was a prostitute. Her attitude to Jesus is vividly revealed by her behavior. The social customs of that ancient and Eastern world were far different from our own. It was not unusual for people to enter into a house where a banquet was taking place. We have to observe how bold this particular woman was, however: a widely known sinner entering a strict Pharisee's house. She brought with her not common olive oil but a very costly jar of perfume, intending probably to anoint Jesus' head. In the ancient Near East, this was a valuable ministry, to soothe and protect skin dried and often cracked because of the climate.

The scenario Luke paints seems to be this. According to the custom of the day, Jesus would have been reclining around a low table, with one hand supporting his head and the other picking up the food, while his feet would have extended out behind. Drawing near to him this woman was overwhelmed with emotion—I suppose because of a combination of her burden over sin and the sheer joy for the presence of Christ. Luke tells us, "She began to wet his feet with her tears." This shows us how intense were her emotions. "Then she wiped them with her hair, kissed them and poured perfume on them" (Luke 7:38). This reveals a tenderness and intimate care that is unusual for us but shows that her heart was melted for Jesus, so that she thought only of him with total abandonment.

The question is What brought this woman to Jesus? And the answer is obvious. She found in him something that won her over, with a total loss of self-consciousness and a complete desire to be with him and serve him. This was a woman, without doubt, who knew little but scorn in the world. She was well acquainted with being used and rejected. It is beautiful, therefore, to see how comfortable she was in the presence of Christ. Here was a man who could be trusted completely, who would receive her trust not in order to use her, not for his callous gain, but for her blessing. Imagine what that would have meant to a woman like this!

No wonder that she came to Jesus with such a release of emotion! Here was One who would not treat her as others did, others who cast her out except when it was convenient to their lusts. Surely you know that for every sinful woman so despised by society there are many men who are quite respectable but who use and scorn her, accepting her only to degrade and destroy her. Obviously this woman saw something completely different in Jesus, something overwhelmingly beautiful in her eyes, utterly captivating to her heart. She found in Jesus love, agape love, the love that is of God and is pure and radiant and warm and safe and good. That is what brought her to Jesus, and it brought her body, mind, and soul.

There are two kinds of people, and Luke illustrates this by these two representative people and their interaction with Jesus. There are the Pharisees, and there are the "sinners." The Pharisee is coldly stand-offish to Jesus, even at the dinner table, while the sinful woman is powerfully drawn to him. She embraces him with tender love and gives to him out of eager devotion. Already we are learning something important, as Harry Ironside relates: "We look down, perhaps, on those in sin and say, 'Thank God we are not like them.' But we little realize how close some of them are to the kingdom of heaven; closer than those who are self-righteous."[1]

A Telling Parable

The focal point of this passage comes by means of the Pharisee's response to this tender scene. I think we can picture it all too well. There is the smug religious formalist on one side of the table. On the other is a relaxed Jesus, allowing this woman to minister to him so lovingly. Luke 7:39 picks up the story, "When the Pharisee who had invited him saw this, he said to himself, 'If this man were a prophet, he would know who is touching him and what kind of woman she is—that she is a sinner.'"

There is a dual condemnation here. The Pharisee concludes from what he sees that, first, Jesus must not be a prophet, lacking such judgment and insight as this scene demonstrates. Second, his condemning thoughts perfectly match those Jesus described in Luke 7:34. The self-righteous looked upon his easy fellowship with the worst of sinners and complained, "Here is a glutton and a drunkard, a friend of tax collectors and 'sinners'."

In Jesus' response there is considerable irony, especially in that it shows he does have prophetic ability. But the sinner he is prophetically scanning is not the woman but the Pharisee. "Simon," Jesus answered in response to the man's thoughts, "I have something to tell you." "Tell me, teacher," he said. Jesus replied with this parable that is at the heart of our passage:

> "Two men owed money to a certain moneylender. One owed him five hundred denarii, and the other fifty. Neither of them had the money to pay him back, so he canceled the debts of both. Now which of them will love him more?" Simon replied, "I suppose the one who had the bigger debt canceled." "You have judged correctly," Jesus said. (Luke 7:41–43)

There are two things I want to highlight about this parable, first an assumption and second an observation. The assumption is that there is really only one kind of person, namely, those who are in debt to God. "All have sinned," the Bible says, "and fall short of the glory of God" (Rom. 3:23). Yes, there may be some difference in the magnitude of the problem—even a tenfold difference—but both men in the parable are in debt to God, and neither has the resources to repay. This assumption, this statement of universal sin, is essential to the gospel proclamation. Donald Grey Barnhouse observed this:

The whole scheme of redemption presupposes that man is a fallen being. Christ came to seek and to save the lost. He was announced as the Saviour of sinners. His advent and work have no meaning or value but on the assumption that we are guilty, for He came to save His people from their sins; to die the Just for the unjust; to bear our sins in His own body on the tree. Those who have no sin need no Saviour; those who do not deserve death, need no Redeemer. As the doctrine of redemption pervades the Scriptures, so does the doctrine of the universal sinfulness of men.[2]

There is only one kind of person, and there is only one kind of salvation, that which is offered to sinners who confess their guilt and need. Jesus assumes this in his parable, and yet it is their unwillingness to accept this fact that accounts for so many rejecting him and his gospel. It is in this sense that there are two kinds of people—not that there are sinners and the righteous, but rather sinners who will confess and be saved and sinners who will not. If you are the kind of person who will not confess your sin, you cannot be saved. All the proud self-righteousness you can muster will not make you any less a sinner; it will make you more of one. It will make you the kind of person who is not forgiven and cannot be saved.

That is the assumption Jesus makes in his parable, and it is accompanied by an important observation. The two people had one thing in common—the fact of their debt—but there was a difference in the magnitude of their debt. "Now which of them," Jesus asked, "will love the man who canceled their debt more?" "I suppose," the Pharisee sheepishly replied, "the one who had the bigger debt canceled." "You have judged correctly," Jesus answered (Luke 7:42–43).

Jesus' observation, arrived at by this question and answer, is that our affection for the forgiver is shaped by the size of the debt we had owed. We always want to be careful not to make Jesus' parables say more than they intend to. This parable is not a comprehensive portrait of salvation, nor does it assume that this Pharisee's sins were forgiven along with the woman's. The point is to show that great love flows from the realization of a great debt that has been forgiven.

In making this point, Jesus more than implies that what pleases God, what motivates God in redemption, is his desire for this loving gratitude. That is a vital insight for us. What is the right response to the forgiveness of our sins? What kind of heart attitude does God seek in us? The answer is here. God wants us to love him much and so he is eager to forgive us much. Paul writes in Romans 11:32 that "God has bound all men over to disobedience so that he may have mercy on them all." The reason is that the God who is love would be loved.

This is the test of our real grasp of theology and biblical truth, not our ability to recite answers and quote Scriptures, but the gratitude we feel and the love we direct toward our God. This is what he seeks and desires, as taught by Jesus in the great commandment that sums up them all: "'Love the Lord your God with all your heart and with all your soul and with all your mind.' This is the first and greatest commandment" (Matt. 22:37–38).

The Necessity of Love

Our passage makes a clear and bold statement regarding the necessity of love for everyone who would be saved. After quizzing the Pharisee, Jesus pressed this truth upon him:

"Do you see this woman? I came into your house. You did not give me any water for my feet, but she wet my feet with her tears and wiped them with her hair. You did not give me a kiss, but this woman, from the time I entered, has not stopped kissing my feet. You did not put oil on my head, but she has poured perfume on my feet. Therefore, I tell you, her many sins have been forgiven—for she loved much. But he who has been forgiven little loves little." Then Jesus said to her, "Your sins are forgiven." (Luke 7:44–48)

The point is that love for God is necessary to forgiveness, because of its close relationship to saving faith. These verses make three points about this relationship: first, that love is inseparable from faith; second, that love is a test of faith; and third, that love provides an assurance of faith.

First, we see *the inseparability of faith in Christ and love for Christ*. Jesus makes this plain in Luke 7:47, 50. In the first verse he says to the Pharisee, "I tell you, her many sins have been forgiven—for she loved much." In the second, Jesus says to her, "Your faith has saved you; go in peace." It is clear that this woman was justified, that is, forgiven, not by kissing or pouring perfume but by faith, just as every other sinner is saved only by faith. Paul writes in Ephesians 2:8–9, "It is by grace you have been saved, through faith—and this not from yourselves, it is the gift of God—not by works, so that no one can boast." This woman was not saved by the merit of her love but by the saving work of Christ, received by faith alone.

Nonetheless, so closely related are faith in Christ and love for Christ that Jesus can freely say to the Pharisee, "Her many sins are forgiven—for she loved much." Alexander Maclaren helpfully explains:

Faith and love have the same object, and are all but contemporaneous. Wherever a man lays hold of Jesus Christ by faith, there cannot but spring up in his heart love to Christ; and there is no love without faith. So that we may almost say that faith and love are but the two throws of the shuttle, the one in the one direction and the other in the other.[3]

John Owen adds, speaking of saving faith: "A spiritual sight of Christ will fill the heart with love for him. So, if any one does not love Christ that person has never seen Christ and does not know him at all."[4]

What is it about faith that necessitates such love? It is the content of faith; it is the work of Christ for us that we receive by faith that causes us to love him so. It is the cross, upon which he died for us, that is not only the handhold of our faith but also the fuel for our spiritual flame of love. The apostle John explains, "We love because he first loved us" (1 John 4:19). Romans 5:8 tells us, "God demonstrates his own love for us in this: While we were still sinners, Christ died for us."

We are not saved by our love, not forgiven by our love. We are forgiven by God's love, by the saving work of Christ, who paid the debt of our sin. But the faith that receives Christ as Savior also loves him as Savior and Lord. Therefore Arthur Pink can write:

The saints are those who love God. Their creeds may differ in minor details, their ecclesiastical relations may vary in outward form, their gifts and graces may be very unequal; yet, in this particular there is an essential unity. They all believe in Christ, they all love God. They love Him for the gift of the Savior; they love Him as a Father in whom they may confide; they love Him for His personal excellencies, His holiness, wisdom, and faithfulness.[5]

There is only one kind of Christian, one who loves God. Since that is true, it follows that *love is also a test of faith.* That is exactly how Jesus employs it in this passage:

> Do you see this woman? I came into your house. You did not give me any water for my feet, but she wet my feet with her tears and wiped them with her hair. You did not give me a kiss, but this woman, from the time I entered, has not stopped kissing my feet. You did not put oil on my head, but she has poured perfume on my feet. (Luke 7:44–46)

The point is not that Simon had a weak faith that won him only a little forgiveness. The point was that Simon did not have faith, as was patently demonstrated by his lovelessness to Christ. The apostle John emphasized this as a test of faith in his first epistle, writing: "Everyone who loves has been born of God and knows God. Whoever does not love does not know God, because God is love" (1 John 4:7–8).

If love is a test of faith, how, then, do I know that I love God? Charles Spurgeon, in a sermon on this text, offered two diagnostic questions, the first of which is Do I think about God? He writes:

> Thoughts fly that way in which the heart moves. I do not say that we are always thinking of those we love; but I do say that our thoughts will fly that way when they can. . . . A man may, in the busy time of

day, think about fifty things; but let him be free from pressing labor and care, and he returns to his love as birds fly to their nests at night. His thought flies to Jesus, because Jesus is the home of his heart. If your hearts love God, your thoughts will run to him as the rivers run to the sea. . . . But where there is no thought of God, there is no love to him.[6]

The second question is Do I do anything for God? This is a diagnostic Jesus gave, saying to his disciples, "If you love me, you will obey what I command" (John 14:5).

Surely, then, if we never do anything for God, we cannot say we love him. Love, by its nature, gives and does. So let me ask you: Do you do anything for God? Do you refrain from sin because it grieves God? If you love God, you find sin sinful because it is sin against him, the holy God who is light and love. Let me ask other questions: Do you sacrifice for and serve God's church? Do you honor the Lord's day? Do you believe and study his Book? Do you love and serve his people? If the answers are no, then it is a matter of fact that you do not love God, and therefore that you do not know him by faith and you are not saved or forgiven.

If you do not think of God, if you do nothing for God, then you are like this Pharisee, whom we do well to remember. Oh, he was religious, but he did not love the Lord, and he did not love the Lord because he had not seen and believed and trusted the truth about Jesus. And for that, despite all his outward piety and good works, he was not saved but stood to perish in his sins.

Love is inseparable from faith and is a test of faith. But *love is also a great assurance of faith.* How many of us tremble for the weakness of our faith, for the burden we feel of our sin, for our frequent infidelity to Jesus. Yet we can say with confidence, "I know this—I love the Lord!" "I have many evil thoughts roaming in my mind, but among them are thoughts of my heavenly home, and my sweet and loving Savior." "I am too well aware of my numerous sins, but I can say that I have and do turn from sin out of love for Jesus. I may not be an exemplary member of the church, but I love the church. I may not represent the Bible very well, but it is my Book, the book of my life and my heart and my trust. And I love the people of God, I pray for them, weep with them, hope for them. I love to see them and be with them. I miss them when away. They are my people, because their God is my God."

If you can say that, however weak your faith, however faint your love, you are forgiven. You love the Lord. How much must you love him? If you love him at all, really love him, it is only because he has poured his love out into you, because you are born again by the Spirit of truth and of love, because your faith has blossomed into the flower of love, a flower that is destined to bloom and grow.

How Can I Love Him?

That brings us to our final point, which is this: Who will love him most? Another way to put this is How can I love him more? The answer is plainly set forth in these two kinds of people. It is not the Pharisee who loves Jesus more, not him who thinks his debt small and his forgiveness of little account. No, it is those like this sinful woman, who know all too well how deep is their debt and therefore how high is the love of their Savior. Surely this is why Jesus later would say to Pharisees like this man Simon: "I tell you the truth, the tax collectors and the prostitutes are entering the kingdom of God ahead of you" (Matt. 21:31).

How am I to love Christ more? Spurgeon cautions:

> Do not try to pump yourselves up into a certain degree of love to Christ by some extraordinary means. Go and live with him, meditate upon him continually, picture to yourself his sufferings for you, and then you will love him—it will become easy to you, and he will lift up your hearts.[7]

Specifically, if you would love Christ you must know your sin. Without the lens of your sin, his grace will not come into focus. Of course the opposite is equally true, that without the protection of his grace we cannot stand the truth about our sin. This passage, then, is a wonderful exhortation to you to accept and confess your sin, perhaps for the first time, because it shows you how tender and loving is our Savior. He is always ready to forgive those who come in faith.

This is how we learn to love the Lord: In the light of his grace we view our sin and through our sin we see how marvelous his grace is. All of this takes place at the cross, where the eyes of our faith behold a wonderful Savior, and like this woman we are enraptured with the presence of Jesus. We are eager to bring costly perfume just to anoint his head. We rain our tears upon his feet and wipe them with our hair.

Every one of us should say and pray, "I wish I had a greater appreciation of my sin and sinfulness; it is essential to my spiritual vitality. I long to be, out of all this great congregation, the one who sees my sin the clearest and most." That is not morbid self-loathing but the companion to this cry, "Oh that I could know the width and length and height and depth of the love of God in Christ that saved me." To know this is to know peace and joy and the movement of a great mainspring of grateful love.

Isn't it wonderful to realize what this passage is saying? What God wants from us is our love. Think of what that meant to this woman! Think of what it means to you. God loves you and wants not your money, not your labor, not your servitude. The Lord omnipotent, the King of heaven, needs none of these, but what he wants is your heart. He is glad to forgive you more and more to have you love him more. Do not think God reluctant to bestow his grace on you, but realize that he is jealous for your love, tender in his affectionate pursuit of your heart. He has demonstrated this once for all at the cross, of which J. I. Packer writes:

> The measure of love is how much it gives, and the measure of the love of God is the gift of his only Son to be made man, and to die for sins, and so to become the one mediator who can bring us to God. No wonder Paul speaks of God's love as "great," and surpassing knowledge! (Eph. 2:4, 3:19).[8]

Look at the last two verses of our passage. Jesus knows what is going on in Simon the Pharisee's heart. His ears hear what is told to us in Luke 7:49: "The other guests began to say among themselves, 'Who is this who even forgives sins?'" These are people, this is an accusation, that will ultimately arise to condemn him to death. Yet Jesus has eyes only for her, for the sinner who has loved him in gratitude for his grace. Jesus gave his attention not to the Pharisee, not to the crowd, but to the woman, oblivious to the threat against himself, and gently ministered to her as she went back out into the world, comforting her as she returned to the scene of her struggle and travail.

There are two kinds of people in this world, and they cannot be told apart by the clothes they wear, by their reputations in the world, by wealth or health or beauty. But in heaven they are known according to their love for Christ and his for them. There are those who belong to Jesus and those who do not. And to his own, as to this woman, Jesus gently says: "Your faith has saved you; go in peace."

That is a wonderful Savior and Lord. How then are you to love him? You do not have to become perfect. You, like this heart-melted woman, do not have to clean up your reputation. You come to him just as you are, a sinner in need of saving grace, a debtor in need of pardon, a believer accepted freely by the Savior who loves you and gave himself for your sins. How do you love Jesus? You simply come to him, as the sinner that you are, but as the kind of sinner who loves him who loves you so.

Jesus and the Little Children

Mark 10:13–16

When Jesus saw this, he was indignant. He said to them, "Let the little children come to me, and do not hinder them, for the kingdom of God belongs to such as these." (Mark 10:14)

One thing that is being impressed upon us through these studies of encounters with Jesus is how attractive Jesus was to those who observed him. In our last study, a woman tainted for her sin was so drawn to Jesus that she barged into a Pharisee's house to wash his feet. In earlier studies we saw how a depraved tax collector left everything immediately when called to follow Jesus and how a Samaritan woman ran to her neighbors to tell about a Jew she just had met. Jesus, we have seen, was especially attractive to outcasts and those who are hopelessly lost in sin apart from his grace. But there were others who were attracted to him, such as the scholar Nicodemus and even the callous governor, Pontius Pilate, who would declare, "I find no basis for a charge against him" (John 19:4).

Jesus is altogether lovely, sweet and attractive as no other person. It is striking to realize that while you can find people to doubt Jesus, to deny his claims, to reject his divinity and refuse his gospel, it is almost impossible to find someone who objects to him as a person. I do not believe that I have ever encountered a soul who thought Jesus anything but virtuous and good and admirable. I realize there are a few, like Friedrich Nietschze, who in their warped thinking find Jesus despicable. But I have never met anyone who, if you talked to him or her, would profess other than that Jesus was a good man. He was the finest man ever, most would even agree.

William Barclay tells the story of an Indian man who was converted and cast out of his house. None of his Hindu family members would accept any contact with him, except that his mother would secretly see him from time to time. Despite his witness, she never would convert, nor did she ever accept his decision. Once, however, she admitted that while pregnant with him she had met a Christian missionary who gave her a New Testament. She read it often, she still did, and while she was carrying him in her womb she often wished that she would bear a son who would be like this man Jesus.[1] Jesus is the rose of Sharon and the lily of the valley; to meet him or even to read of him is to admire his beauty of spirit and wish others were like him.

But I think there is no greater testimony to Jesus' lovely character than the words that begin our present passage, "People were bringing little children to Jesus to have him touch them" (Mark 10:13). The mothers, and perhaps fathers as well, were bringing their little children to him. Luke's account makes it plain that these were babies. What a measure of a man's character this is! Would mothers eagerly bring their infants into just anyone's arms? That they so wanted Jesus to hold and to bless and to pray for their babies testifies to his gentleness, as is said of him in Isaiah: "A bruised reed he will not break" (Isa. 42:3). It testifies to his peacefulness and purity of heart, "like a lily among thorns" says the Song of Songs (Song 2:2).

The Christian writer George Macdonald is quoted as saying that "no man could be a follower of Jesus, if the children were afraid to play at his door."[2] Those who are children of God are lovers of children and, because of the Spirit of Christ at work in their hearts, are usually loved by children in return. If that is true of the Christian, how much more is it true of the Christ.

This encounter, like the ones before, shows us the attractiveness of Jesus. But it also, like the others, involves a controversy, a confrontation this time between Christ and his disciples. As we will see, Jesus reproves them and uses the occasion to make three great statements we will consider. They are a statement about ministry, a statement about children, and a statement about faith.

A Statement about Ministry

The passage begins, as I have said, with these people who brought their little children to the Lord Jesus. We have already discussed what is probably the main reason for their coming, his loveliness of person. But there were considerable deterrents as well, most specifically his bad reputation among the religious authorities. This encounter takes place near the end of Jesus' earthly ministry, during his march from Galilee to Jerusalem and the cross. Almost every other passage at this stage in the Gospels involves a confrontation with the religious authorities. Therefore it was not safe to associate with Jesus. People were being put out of the synagogue merely for being healed by him, and things were likely to get worse.

It was extraordinary, then, for these mothers to mark their little children by association with a man who shortly would be executed as a criminal. Obviously there was a great amount of faith involved. They had seen what his hands were able to do. They had no doubt witnessed the healing of the sick, the cleansing of lepers, the casting out of evil spirits, and despite all the risk of public scandal they brought their children into Jesus' hands to be blessed. That is a great statement of faith, just as Jesus said, "Whoever acknowledges me before men, I will also acknowledge him before my Father in heaven" (Matt. 10:32).

We find, however, that the disciples were displeased by what was taking place. Mark tells us they rebuked these parents and tried to stop what was happening. But "when Jesus saw this, he was indignant. He said to them, 'Let the little children come to me, and do not hinder them' " (Mark 10:14). In this we find a great statement about true Christian ministry.

There are a number of suggestions to explain the disciples' action. The first is that they thought it beneath Jesus' dignity to minister to children and of too little importance for him to be bothered. This is not an outlandish suggestion, for if the disciples would spend so much time arguing about who among themselves was the greatest (Mark 9:33–34), then they would be prone to thinking of others in terms of their worldly importance.

But the Christian ministry is not just for the powerful and those who are useful but also for the smallest and weakest. It is to those who are poor, who are meek, who mourn, that Christ gives his blessing (Matt. 5:3–5). It would be remarkable for those involved in ministry to think little children unimportant and of little value. Such thinking would show a truly skewed vision not just of ministry but also of life in general. And yet Christian churches often sin by showing preference to the powerful and rich while despising the weak. If that was the disciples' motive, we see why Jesus was indignant toward them.

Another possible explanation is that the disciples did not want Jesus distracted by individual people from his more important public ministry, work such as praying and teaching and disputing with the Pharisees. But Jesus thought otherwise. He makes a statement that we need to take to heart. On the one hand we must remember that Christian pastors are called specifically to the ministry of prayer and the Word. This is what the apostles taught and modeled in the early church. Acts 6 tells of a controversy that had arisen about the distribution of food. This was an important matter, but instead of giving their time to it the apostles appointed the first deacons. In Acts 6:2–4, they give their reason, making an important statement for all ministers of the Word: "It would not be right for us to neglect the ministry of the word of God in order to wait on tables. . . . We . . . will give our attention to prayer and the ministry of the word." Whenever men ordained to teach break that pattern, neglecting time apart for prayer and study, the church suffers.

At the same time, however, we have to observe that in all the Gospel accounts we never read of Jesus turning anyone away. His work was undoubtedly much more spiritual than the various committees and other meetings any church leader gives a great deal of time to today, and yet Jesus gladly allowed people to interfere. People are not a distraction from the real work of ministry but are the sole object of that ministry. Therefore a true Christian ministry must say what Jesus said, not just about children but about everyone in need, "Let them come, and do not hinder them."

Another suggestion for the disciples' behavior does them far more credit, namely, that they were concerned for Jesus' fatigue and distress. This was during a most difficult and demanding period of his life on earth. He was frequently talking about the cross, disputing with opponents, and sacrificing his energy for healing the many sick people. But if that was their motive, understandable as it is, the disciples were reproved all the same.

It is every Christian minister's calling to expend himself for the flock of God, and that was especially Christ's calling on earth. We remember that these same disciples tried to dissuade Jesus from the cross, apart from which we would have no salvation. But Jesus reproved them, saying in Matthew 20:28, "The Son of Man came not to be served, but to serve, and to give his life as a ransom for many." Jesus did not have an iron curtain around his person or his time or his life. Neither should any minister of Christ, serving in his name.

Finally, the disciples might have opposed the bringing of these children on the grounds that they could derive no benefit from Jesus' ministry. This is the kind of thing you often hear today, usually associated with an unbiblical idea of an age of accountability, which wrongly relates developmental immaturity with an inability to know and trust Jesus Christ. If the disciples thought the children could not benefit from Christ's blessing, they were forgetting that it is Christ's work that is of first importance in salvation. If Jesus heals you, you are healed; and if Jesus blesses you, you are blessed. In this regard, Jesus' response made a clear statement regarding children, and to that we now will turn.

A Statement about Children

Mark tells us that "people were bringing little children to Jesus to have him touch them." Matthew gives a little more detail, writing, "Little children were brought to Jesus for him to place his hands on them and pray for them" (Matt. 19:13).

This was anything but a trivial gesture. Here was the Lord of the covenant with children of the covenant people. He laid his hands on them and blessed them, just as the patriarchs of the covenant blessed their children, as Isaac blessed Jacob. Then he prayed for them. We are not to think of his actions as trivial or trite. These children were, as the song tells us, "precious in his sight." Jesus therefore blessed these children, and so they were blessed indeed.

There are three things we want to make sure we know about children. The first is that *children are sinners in need of saving grace*. They are not innocent, and if you doubt that I invite you to visit any church nursery and stick your head in the door for about five minutes. The children are received by Jesus not because they are innocent but because they are not. They are the seed of sinful Adam, whose corruption and guilt have been poured into their veins from conception. As David said in Psalm 51:5,

Surely I was sinful at birth,
    sinful from the time my mother conceived me.

Had these children not been sinners, then it would have been a waste of Jesus' time to bless them, for his was a ministry of salvation for sinners.

The second thing we must realize about children is that *they have spiritual potential and teachability*. Jesus says in Mark 10:14, "The kingdom of God belongs to such as these." If you spend much time with children in the church you will find that to be the case. We want to assert the Bible's general teaching about man's spiritual inability. "No one can come to me," Jesus said, "unless the Father who sent me draws him" (John 6:44). But within that constraint, we should observe that children have a relatively high spiritual perception, and their hearts can be drawn to God more easily than can the hearts of adults. Although they are sinners, they are not yet as well trained in unbelief. Belief in God is quite natural to children; it makes sense within their world of wonder and of joy. Until I became a father and observed children intimately, I would never have guessed how spiritually perceptive even very little children can be.

The implication of this is seen in Jesus' words: "Let the little children come to me, and do not hinder them" (Mark 10:14). Children therefore must be evangelized and discipled. We do so by the ordinary means of grace, diligently and wisely applied. We preach and teach them the Word of God. Mothers talk to their children about the gospel and lead them into the arms of the Savior. Fathers pray for and with their children and pastor their souls unto salvation. We together in the whole church must diligently apply every biblical means to convert and then lead our children into maturity in the faith. J. C. Ryle wisely writes:

> We must never allow ourselves to suppose that little children's souls may be safely let alone. . . . They are

never too young to learn evil and sin. They are never too young to receive religious impressions. They think in their childish way about God, and their souls, and a world to come, far sooner and far more deeply than most people are aware. . . . We cannot begin too soon to endeavour to bring them to Christ.[3]

Children should be exposed to the reality of sin, the offer of forgiveness, and a relationship to God through Jesus Christ from the absolutely earliest age. My experience with my children is that by age two they are able to learn Bible verses and hymns and to study theology through the children's catechism. My four-year-old daughter not only keeps up with our regimen but also continually surprises me by her spiritual advancement. When she was three, she not only knew much Scripture but applied it to her circumstances and prayed on her own initiative. I am very much aware of how far my three small children have yet to go, and I approach the coming years with prayer and a great sense of dependence on God's faithfulness. But I also approach them with faith, knowing that Jesus calls little children to himself.

The point is that little children are spiritually able sinners, and we must teach, evangelize, and disciple them. Bishop Ryle rightly concludes:

> It is the bounden duty of every Christian congregation to make provision for the spiritual training of its children. . . . No church can be regarded as being in a healthy state which neglects its younger members. . . . Such a church shows plainly that it has not the mind of Christ.[4]

Children are messy, they are noisy, they are frustrating and difficult. They are not, however, a nuisance in the church. We must train them to participate in the worship service, to sing hymns and attend upon the preached Word of God. James Montgomery Boice put it well in an article about children:

> The goal we should have with our children is to bring them up to the level of the adults—that is, to enable them to begin to function on an adult level in their relationships to God. . . . Even if they can-not follow what goes on at first, our task is to teach them so they both can and will.[5]

I must say, however, that if the children's literature and especially the videos coming out of the evangelical media are any indication, we are falling far short of evangelizing and teaching our children. Most children's material does the very thing Jesus was so indignant about—they keep the little children from him, at least from any biblical notion of Jesus. Far too often Jesus is presented not as the Lord of glory and Savior of sinners but as one of the *Rugrats*, to cite a particularly obnoxious children's cartoon that is sadly popular today. In place of gospel truth there is often only moral sentiment combined with a vague exhortation to prayer. Yes, children should learn the stories of the Bible, but they also need the doctrine the Bible gives with and through the stories. They need to learn about God and his attributes and the saving work of Christ.

There is a third thing for us to notice about children in this passage, namely, that *they are connected to Jesus through the faith of their parents.* People object to this teaching in our individualistic age, but nothing is more in conformity to the mind of Scripture. Israelite boys were circumcised on their eighth day, receiving the sign of the covenant. Paul, in 1 Corinthians 7:14, states in the most casual way that the children of believers are holy. That doesn't mean they are saved but that before God they are different from other children. In Ephesians 6, Paul directs his apostolic command to children, directing them to obey their parents in the Lord, plainly assuming an existing relationship to God. Every covenant in Scripture includes believers with their children. This is true of the new covenant, as Peter preached on the day of Pentecost: "The promise is for you and your children" (Acts 2:38). How natural it is, therefore, to see Jesus receiving these babes from the hands of their believing parents.

This logic explains why the infant children of believers are to be baptized, just as Christ received and blessed them with prayer. He demands that they be brought to him; he says that such are those who receive the kingdom of heaven. Jesus prayed for them, and it is hard to imagine that the Savior failed to pray for their salvation. We don't know that any or all of these babies went on to saving faith. But we should expect that they did. God promises to be our God and our children's God. They are members of Christ's church through us, and so we baptize them, expecting that they will be saved and laboring to that end in faith.

This passage does not explicitly teach infant baptism. Nor does it teach that believers' children are automatically saved, just as we do not teach that all who are baptized— either as children or as adults—are automatically saved. Our children, like us, must believe or they will be lost, for salvation is through faith alone. But nothing here speaks against infant baptism, and everything commends the idea. It is hard to explain how Christian children should be kept from the sacrament that identifies people with Jesus, when he expressly commands, "Let them come to me, and do not hinder them, for the kingdom of God belongs to such as these."

Whatever we think of infant baptism, we are bound by this passage to see the great statement Jesus is making about children, who are sinners, who are spiritually capable, and who are related to Christ through the faith of their parents.

A Statement about Faith

Finally Jesus uses this encounter to make a great statement about the character of saving faith. Matthew's and Luke's Gospels give a longer statement, reading, "The kingdom of God belongs to such as these. I tell you the truth, anyone who will not receive the kingdom of God like a little child will never enter it" (Luke 18:16–17).

The expression "such as these" clearly indicates that the children provide a representative picture of simple trust and dependent faith. R. C. Sproul makes a helpful comment about this:

> So often this passage is interpreted to mean that Christians are always to have a child-like faith, in the sense that we ought always to keep our faith very simple, and not allow it to be encumbered by diligent study of the Word of God. However, there is a difference between a childlike faith and a childish faith. A childish faith chooses to remain immature, but a childlike faith, the kind that Jesus calls for, is a simple, confident trust in, and dependence on our heavenly Father. . . . When it comes to our salvation, we must have a childlike

trust in God's mercy and grace or we will miss the kingdom of God.[6]

I think of three things that a child's faith looks for. The first is *protection*. My home is located on one busy street that nearby intersects a dangerous street, in terms of the speed and volume of automobile traffic. We do not really have a yard, and across the street at this intersection is a park where my children like to play. Therefore we often walk along this stream of high-velocity steel and rubber. Particularly as we draw near to this scary intersection, my children eagerly grasp my hand. Their eyes are searching for me, looking for reassurance in my protective presence and control.

So too does a believer's faith look to our heavenly Father and to Jesus Christ for protection. In spiritual attack it is to him that we cry, even instinctively. In temptation we call out to him, lifting the shield of faith in the Lord. When sickness or death or any other threat draws near, our faith is very much that described in Psalm 23:4:

Even though I walk
through the valley of the shadow of death,
I will fear no evil,
for you are with me.

That is the attitude of a child's faith in God; it looks to him in danger and finds peace and safety and comfort.

Second, a childlike faith seeks *instruction*. I have already spoken of our duty to teach the gospel to children. What I have not mentioned is how much they love to learn it. How often little children say, "Daddy, show me! Teach me!" Oh, that this would characterize adults' approach to

Scripture! A childlike faith is like the one that speaks to God in Psalm 119:

> Teach me knowledge and good judgment,
>   for I believe in your commands. (v. 66)

> Your word is a lamp to my feet
>   and a light for my path. (v. 105)

Someday soon, I know, my little children will be less childlike, less eager to listen to their father. But the little child's faith, which Christ commends, looks up with eyes wide and bright, longing to hear and learn from his or her trusted parent. This is the faith, Jesus says, that receives the kingdom of God.

Let me observe that liberal theology, be it ancient liberalism, modern liberalism, or today's growing evangelical liberalism, is marked by the absence of this kind of childlike faith. What makes liberal theology liberal is its confidence in its own knowledge and in the wisdom that comes from the world. It is confident in the validity of its opinions and judgments but skeptical about the clarity with which God's Word can or does speak. It doubts the authority of Scripture while highly esteeming the findings of human scholarship. How far this is from the little child's faith, which gladly accepts its ignorance, longs to be taught, and trusts the authority of the Father.

Finally, a child's faith looks to its parent for *approval and blessing*. Children crave these things from fathers, just as we are to crave our heavenly Father's pleasure in Christ. In this we are not disappointed, as Zephaniah 3:17 tells us:

> The LORD your God is with you,
>   he is mighty to save.

> He will take great delight in you,
>> he will quiet you with his love,
>> he will rejoice over you with singing.

If you look to the heavenly Father through faith in Christ, you will find his approval, because Christ has won it once for all. You will also begin a lifetime of learning to please God, as he works his will and his ways into your life.

I am reminded of a scene played out on countless little league baseball parks every summer. There is a young boy or girl, desperately longing for a base hit, simply for the approving look of a father who sits there in the stands. I remember my father coming home from work to throw baseballs to me, to coach me with the bat, teaching me to keep my eye on the ball, and then cheering for me when I succeeded as if it all had been my doing.

In just that way our heavenly Father pours himself out into us for that which he longs and desires. "It is God who works in you to will and to act according to his good purpose," Paul writes (Phil. 2:13). And whenever we do his will, he rejoices as a Father, praising us as though it all had been our doing. It is that look of joy on the Father's face that is the goal of the childlike faith that Jesus loves. It is our highest privilege and greatest pleasure.

That is what it means to have a childlike Christian faith: to look to God for protection, from sin and guilt but also from the dangers and trials of this world; to humbly sit beneath his Word for instruction; and finally to live our lives for the sake of his pleasure, longing to see the beaming smile of our loving Father. The faith that seeks these things finds them through Jesus Christ and receives the kingdom of God.

Safe in His Hands

My youngest child is a four-month-old baby boy, probably the age of many of these children Jesus held lovingly in his hands. Our little son cannot do very much, just as we cannot do very much when it comes to the matter of our salvation. He cannot stand, he cannot talk, he cannot feed or defend himself. But he can do what we must do if we are to be saved: he can cry out for help and then grab hold for all he is worth. Surely Jesus had this too in mind when speaking of the faith of little children. There they were nestled up against Jesus' breast, held in all their weakness in the strength of his saving hands and therefore safe within the kingdom of God. One thing a baby can do is to grab and hold on to the one who keeps him safe. And that is what we must do, safe in the hands of Jesus the Savior.

That, in its simplest and most important sense, is what Christian faith is all about, that we would grab hold of the Lord Jesus Christ, resting ourselves upon his power to save. Therefore hold fast to him in faith, and realize that like any good parent, our heavenly Father is also holding on to you with diligent parental care. You can trust him like a child, knowing that through Jesus Christ you are protected and adored and that God will lead you through this life. If you believe that, as you believe that, you will have the peace of a child in the hands of his or her father. Therefore Jesus says to us, even now, "Let the little children come to me, and do not hinder them, for the kingdom of God belongs to such as these."

Jesus and the Rich Young Man

Mark 10:17–31

Jesus looked at him and loved him. "One thing you lack," he said. "Go, sell everything you have and give to the poor, and you will have treasure in heaven. Then come, follow me." At this the man's face fell. He went away sad, because he had great wealth. Jesus looked around and said to his disciples, "How hard it is for the rich to enter the kingdom of God!"
(Mark 10:21–23)

The biblical accounts of Jesus' life are called Gospels because they are good news. In our studies of encounters with Jesus we have seen the effects of his ministry, and it has been good news indeed. He has reached out to the Samaritans, raised the lame, called sinners into the kingdom of God.

This passage in Mark 10, however, strikes a much different note. In all the Bible I think there are few more tragic accounts, few sadder and in many ways disturbing than the encounter between Jesus and the rich young man.

The reason I say this is that there are few people more commendable than this man. He was earnest and respectable, and he came humbly seeking salvation from Jesus Christ. But there are also few more regrettable people. Here was a man who had everything, except the one thing needed to enter into eternal life. For all these reasons, this encounter that turns out so poorly is also rich in instruction for all who would receive heavenly treasures from Jesus.

A Fatal Ignorance

The man we are considering approached Jesus in a manner we certainly want to commend. Mark introduces him: "As Jesus started on his way, a man ran up to him and fell on his knees before him. 'Good teacher,' he asked, 'what must I do to inherit eternal life?'" (Mark 10:17).

The different Gospel accounts provide different details. All present this man as wealthy. Matthew tells us he was young, and Luke states that he was a ruler, which probably means a synagogue leader. This is why he is generally known as the rich young ruler.

What stands out is the difference between him and most of the people who clamored around Jesus. He did not come to Jesus to have some temporal problem fixed. It wasn't a disease or hunger that brought him. He did not come to Jesus to test or accuse him, but he came with the highest of all motives. He came to inquire about eternal life. Even his use of that term, "eternal life," sets him apart from the vast majority who failed to comprehend the point of Jesus' teaching.

It seems this man caught sight of Jesus and he came running, such was the urgency of his concern. He fell before Jesus, addressed him as "good teacher," and asked the question most appropriate to Jesus' ministry. Where others were careless, he was anxious about spiritual matters; while others despised Jesus, he showed the highest degree of reverence. From our perspective, this is perhaps the most promising contact Jesus has had in all of his ministry.

Therefore it is striking to see how sharp was Jesus' reply, while to others he had been mild:

> "Why do you call me good?" Jesus answered. "No one is good—except God alone. You know the commandments: 'Do not murder, do not commit adultery, do not steal, do not give false testimony, do not defraud, honor your father and mother.' " (Luke 10:18–19)

It is not hard to explain why Jesus acted this way. His point was not to deny his own goodness. This is not a refutation of Jesus' perfect sinlessness under the law, and those who make such a claim show only their perverse attitude toward our Lord. The point is obvious: Jesus found something in this young man that must be confronted and challenged, namely, his perspective on salvation. He came to Jesus to learn what works he must do to be saved; while he addressed Jesus as a "good" teacher, the inference is that he hoped to establish himself in a similar light. Matthew's Gospel gives us a slightly different version of Jesus' reply, perhaps to guard against any potential slight against our Lord, but one that also sheds light on the point Jesus was making: " 'Why do you ask me about what is good?' Jesus replied. 'There is only One who is good. If you want to enter life, obey the commandments' " (Matt. 19:17).

Jesus' point was that the man did not need to come to him to discover the works of righteousness, for they were already taught with great clarity in the law. His statement reveals an important truth about Jesus' ministry, namely, that he did not come to teach us right and wrong. Many people want to emphasize Jesus as a moral teacher and good example, to make this the centerpiece of his earthly ministry. Such people usually approach Jesus the way this rich young man did, sure of their goodness and eager to earn their way to salvation. Jesus did teach such things, especially in the Sermon on the Mount, where he showed the true spiritual meaning of the law. But Jesus was not a moralist who thought that good people would do right if they only had a positive example.

You see how this passage refutes the idea. As this encounter makes plain, right and wrong, the works of righteousness God commands, are already made known in the commandments of the law. When asked why he spent time with sinners and not with the good people like this young man, Jesus replied, "It is not the healthy who need a doctor, but the sick. I have not come to call the righteous but sinners" (Mark 2:17). Jesus did not come as a moral teacher but as a Savior for sinners.

Jesus answered the young man's question, therefore, with this: The law tells you what works are required for eternal life. You don't need to ask me but merely to do them. "If you want to enter life, obey the commandments." Mark 10:20 gives the man's reply, a reply that demonstrates his gross self-ignorance: "Teacher," he declared, "all these I have kept since I was a boy."

This young man surely said this with sincerity. Jesus had laid before him the second tablet of the law. These items in Mark 10:19 are the fifth through tenth commandments, those that deal with love toward man, just as the first table deals with love toward God. Jesus probably turned to these because how we respond to people is easier to assess than our attitude toward God.

The young man looked back on his life and honestly, I think, made this positive assessment. He had never killed anyone or committed adultery. He was reared to know that stealing was wrong, as were lying and fraud. If his parents were there, they would have confirmed that he was a good and obedient child. Therefore, with utter sincerity, he replied to Jesus, "All these I have kept since I was a boy."

This young man thought about sin the way we tend to do. We grew up being graded on a relative standard. We didn't have to get 100 percent to pass the class. Even 90 percent puts us in the A range. A 70 percent performance might rate only a C, but that is a passing grade. Only a few people at the end of the scale fail. Our mistake, then, when we consider our performance before God, is that we apply this same system.

What a shock it is, therefore, to learn that God does not use a relative but an absolute standard. He does not grade on a curve, so that you only have to be a little bit better than most people. He grades according to his character, which is perfect. He requires perfection when it comes to the righteous demands of the law. His standard is his perfect holiness, and therefore the law repeatedly says, "Be holy, because I am holy" (Lev. 11:44). The apostle James explains, "Whoever keeps the whole law and yet stumbles at just one point is guilty of breaking all of it" (James 2:10). That is the way God grades us under the law.

I am perfectly confident that according to that standard, this man would not have dared to reply as he did. I feel equally confident asking you to reflect on your conduct, even on the surface of the commandments. Even breaking one commandment, like the ninth, "You shall not lie," places each and every one of us into the category this man was not willing to place himself, namely, that of a sinner.

It is true that Jesus taught a higher principle than the letter of the law, as the Old Testament did before him. In the Sermon on the Mount he pressed home the true and spiritual application of God's commandments. Matthew 5 tells us:

> You have heard that it was said to the people long ago, "Do not murder, and anyone who murders will be subject to judgment." But I tell you that anyone who is angry with his brother will be subject to judgment. . . . You have heard that it was said, "Do not commit adultery." But I tell you that anyone who looks at a woman lustfully has already committed adultery with her in his heart. (Matt. 5:21–22, 27–28)

Jesus told the man, "If you want to enter life, obey the commandments." The only right response would have been to cry, "But the commandments condemn me, for with my hands and especially with my heart I have broken them and stand guilty as charged." The same applies to us. Alexander Maclaren writes:

> How many of us are there who, if ever we cast a careless glance over our lives, are quite satisfied with their external respectability! As long as the chambers that look to the street are fairly clean, many think that all is right. But what is there rotting and festering down in the cellars? Do we ever

go down there with the "candle of the Lord" in our hands? If we do, the ruler's boast, "All these have I kept," will falter into, "All these have I broken."[1]

Mark tells us, "Jesus looked at him" (Mark 10:21). I would not want to be in that situation, kneeling before Jesus Christ protesting my righteousness, with the Son of God gazing upon and into me.

Surprisingly, however, Mark adds, "and Jesus loved him." What a remarkable statement! "Jesus loved him." Jesus obviously appreciated the struggle this man was going through. Although he casually replied that he had kept the law, this young man came to Jesus because he lacked what was needed for eternal life. He did not know the life that is of God and that lasts forever, and he did not know why. Jesus perceived the man's struggle, who came running to ask for eternal life while clinging to the works of the law. Jesus looked into him piercingly but also with compassion and love.

Jesus, we remember, came as a doctor among the sick. Here he applies his lancet directly to the heart of the patient's wound. Jesus saw this conscience seeking relief, coupled with an understanding darkened by ignorance of the first principles of true religion. His words to the man aimed to enlighten this fatal ignorance. " 'One thing you lack,' he said. 'Go, sell everything you have and give to the poor, and you will have treasure in heaven. Then come, follow me' " (Mark 10:21).

Jesus was not establishing a universal principle for salvation, so that salvation is by the good work of selling all your worldly goods. His point was to expose the love of money that was keeping this man from salvation. For others it might be power or beauty or fame or comfort; the point is that there was in this man at least something he held higher than the kingdom of God, something that stood between him and saving faith. By means of this command, Jesus would have him realize that he did not love his neighbor as himself and therefore was not a keeper of the law. He did not love the Lord with all his heart and mind and strength, which is the heart of the law.

Jesus taught, "Where your treasure is, there your heart will be also. . . . You cannot serve both God and Money" (Matt. 6:21, 24). This man reveals his true loyalty. Mark describes what happened succinctly. At Jesus' command, "The man's face fell. He went away sad, because he had great wealth" (Mark 10:22). He turned away from the eternal life he had sought because he possessed great earthly riches, or rather because his great earthly riches possessed him.

What a tragic picture this is. The man had raced to Jesus eager to do whatever would win him salvation. But when exposed to the reality of his sin and the true nature of his heart and its affections, he turned away from salvation, away from the Savior. Jesus showed him something he could not do, and he walked away from eternal life rather than admit his need for saving grace. The only positive thing we can say is that he went away sad, surely with much to think about later. Yet this is not a likely prelude to a later conversion. We hear nothing of this man in Scripture and must conclude that he walked away for good.

We remember that this passage comes right after Jesus' encounter with the little children, and surely the rich young ruler is set in deliberate contrast. He was strong, while the children were weak; he was self-reliant, while they were dependent and trusting. He turned away from the Lord in frustration, while the children nestled peacefully in Jesus' arms. It is an effective contrast: a contrast between self-reliant works and the dependent faith that receives the kingdom of God.

Jesus' Teaching about Salvation

I think Jesus must have followed the man with his eyes for quite some time, only then turning back to employ this encounter to instruct his disciples. In this encounter and in the discussion that followed we learn three things about salvation.

First, we learn that *salvation is through faith and not by works*. This is the principle that governed Jesus' whole treatment of this outwardly righteous man.

Jesus did not allow him to bandy about human goodness, for as Paul would write of mankind, "There is no one who does good, not even one" (Rom. 3:12). Jesus is the lone exception, being the sinless Son of God. But the first thing men and women have to understand about salvation is that they are not good, that their works cannot save them, because they are corrupted by sin.

We go back to the man's question to Jesus, "What must I do to inherit eternal life?" and we see the problem Jesus identified. It is a bit clearer in Matthew's version, which reads, "Teacher, what good thing must I do to get eternal life?" (Matt. 19:16). He was seeking not a way to saving grace but a work by which he might be recompensed.

Proverbs 14:12 tells us,

> There is a way that seems right to a man,
> but in the end it leads to death.

This is that way, the way of merit and of works. Man wants works as the way to salvation, because works bring glory to the one who does them. The Bible proclaims, on the contrary, that salvation is by faith in God and the saving work of Jesus Christ. Salvation is by faith because the holy God does not accept our works, tainted as they are by sin. Isaiah put it best when he said, "All our righteous acts are like filthy rags" (Isa. 64:6). Salvation is also by faith, as Paul says in Romans 4:16, "so that it might be by grace," and thus to the glory of God alone. "For it is by grace you have been saved," he says, "through faith—and this not from yourselves, it is the gift of God—not by works, so that no one can boast" (Eph. 2:8–9).

What is so amazing is that those who would teach salvation by works have historically turned to this passage for support. They see Jesus establishing a way of merit and works for salvation. But how far that is from his intention, and in Mark 10:27 Jesus shuts out any such possibility. "With man," he said, "this is impossible."

"What good works can I do?" This is the religion that has launched a thousand pilgrimages to holy shrines, erected a thousand monasteries, woven thousands of hair shirts, and motivated countless moral crusades. This is the logic that glorifies the goodness of men but does not, cannot, inherit eternal life for sinners.

The apostle Paul once thought this way. He tells us in Philippians 3 that he trusted his many virtues for salvation: "Circumcised on the eighth day, of the people of Israel, of the tribe of Benjamin, a Hebrew of Hebrews; in regard to the law, a Pharisee; as for zeal, persecuting the church; as for legalistic righteousness, faultless" (Phil. 3:5–6). But when Paul met Jesus Christ, he realized that what he thought was his asset column was really filled with liabilities that kept him from salvation. Therefore he concludes:

But whatever was to my profit I now consider loss for the sake of Christ. What is more, I consider everything a loss compared to the surpassing greatness of knowing Christ Jesus my Lord, for whose sake I have lost all things. I consider them rubbish, that I may gain Christ and be found in him, not having a righteousness of my own that comes from the law, but that which is through faith in Christ— the righteousness that comes from God and is by faith. (Phil. 3:7–9)

In this respect it is a great tragedy that this young man turned away from Christ when his sinful love of money was exposed. He could have had eternal life—it was right before him—if only he could have cried, "Lord, I see that I am a sinner! I reject my works and self-righteousness, turning instead to you in faith." There was his great mistake, and it is a mistake you must not make if you are to gain what he lost—forgiveness of sins and eternal life with God. Jesus said to him, "You lack one thing," and surely that one thing included the knowledge that salvation is through faith in Christ alone.

The second point about salvation came when the man had walked away and Jesus turned to his disciples. "How hard it is," he said, "for the rich to enter the kingdom of God!" (Mark 10:23). *Earthly riches*, he says, *are an impediment to salvation*. The Bible notes a good many rich people who were saved—Joseph of Arimathea and surely Nicodemus—but on the whole the rich are underrepresented in the kingdom of salvation. As Paul wrote to the Corinthian believers:

Brothers, think of what you were when you were called. Not many of you were wise by human standards; not many were influential; not many were of noble birth. But God chose the foolish things of the world to shame the wise; God chose the weak things of the world to shame the strong. He chose the lowly things of this world and the despised things—and the things that are not—to nullify the things that are, so that no one may boast before him. (1 Cor. 1:26–29)

It is hard for the rich to esteem the things of heaven above the things of earth. Riches encourage a false sense of power and self-worth and provide broad opportunities for selfishness, which is no doubt why surveys reveal that the poor give away a higher percentage of their income than do the rich. Moreover the danger of money is not only for the rich but also for everyone who longs to be rich and therefore seeks salvation in money.

Jesus used a vivid illustration to show just how difficult it is for the rich to be saved: "It is easier for a camel to go through the eye of a needle than for a rich man to enter the kingdom of God" (Mark 10:25). The camel was the largest beast in the Middle East. The eye of a needle probably refers to the small doorway found alongside most city gates. When the main gates were closed, individuals could squeeze through this little passage. The idea is for us to picture a camel laden with great treasures trying to squeeze through a tiny doorway. Even when most of the riches are removed, leaving only a petty fortune, the animal will not fit. "It is easier for a camel to go through the eye of a needle than for a rich man to enter the kingdom of God." Jesus' point is that neither scenario is possible; in the one case it is a physical impossibility and in the other a spiritual impossibility.

This leads to the third statement our passage makes about salvation, namely, that *saving faith requires self-surrender*. That is what Jesus was pressing on the young man when he demanded that he sell all his possessions. The issue was not about money but his unwillingness to surrender himself to the Lord. That is what is necessary for any of us to attain eternal life, not as a meritorious work but as the character of true and saving faith. Charles Spurgeon put it this way:

> If you would be saved by the blood of Jesus, you are not from this day to choose your own pleasures, not your own ways, nor your own thoughts, nor to serve yourselves, nor live for yourselves or your own aggrandizement. If you would be saved, you must believe what he tells you, do what he bids you, and live only to serve and honour him. . . . He has bought us, not with silver and gold, but with his own precious blood. Surely, then, we should be quite willing to say, "Tis done, the great transaction's done, I am my Lord's and he is mine."[2]

That indeed is more difficult for us than for a camel to fit through the eye of a needle. Jesus presented it not only as hard but also as impossible. "With man this is impossible," he said. "Who then can be saved?" cried the disciples, understanding his point full well. Jesus responded, "With man this is impossible, but not with God; all things are possible with God" (Mark 10:27).

The Power of Saving Grace

This leaves us with one matter to consider from this passage, namely, the power of saving grace for those who have trusted in Jesus. Peter was the first to point to this, crying out, as Matthew's Gospel puts it: "We have left everything to follow you! What then will there be for us?" (Matt. 19:27).

That may not be the noblest sentiment, but it was true. What the rich young man, with all his attainments and outward righteousness was unwilling to do, unable to do, Peter and the others had done. We saw this earlier, in our study of the calling of Peter and his friends, as well as in the calling of Matthew the former tax collector. These disciples, though far less righteous than the rich young man, had achieved what he could not do. They had left everything and followed Jesus.

How had they done what Jesus said is impossible to man? There is our answer. What is impossible to us is possible to God, and therefore their faith and obedience to Christ were the result of God's grace working in them with power. Peter and the others show us that saving grace, working through the faith of the weakest believer, is able to do what the most virtuous humanity cannot accomplish without the saving grace of God.

It will be the same for you. What you could never do out of your strength as a work intended to merit salvation, you can do as a humble believer trusting in Christ. Paul gave the reason in Galatians 2:20: "I have been crucified with Christ and I no longer live, but Christ lives in me." His famous statement from Philippians 4:13 puts it equally well: "I can do everything through him who gives me strength." Here is the rule for the Christian life, as told by Jesus in John 15:5, "I am the vine; you are the branches. If a man remains in me and I in him, he will bear much fruit; apart from me you can do nothing."

Therefore it should be commonplace to see Christians

living by faith on a level unattainable to the unsaved man. Christians should have a mysterious quality as we walk through the world, because of the power for righteousness, peace, and joy that comes from God by faith and is unattainable by any other means.

Peter exclaimed, "We have left everything to follow you! What then will there be for us?" (Matt. 19:27). Jesus replied with a second facet of the power of God's grace, namely, the power to bless and enrich those who follow him. Jesus replied, "No one who has left home or brothers or sisters or mother or father or children or fields for me and for the gospel will fail to receive a hundred times as much in this present age (homes, brothers, sisters, mothers, children and fields—and with them, persecutions) and in the age to come, eternal life" (Mark 10:29–30).

Here too is the mystery of godliness. The Christian holds loss and gain together. Jesus plainly acknowledges that to follow him is to lose homes and families and friends and worldly comforts and satisfactions. To follow him we must take up a cross. And yet through that cross comes the greatest of gains, even on this side of heaven. J. C. Ryle explains:

> They shall have not only pardon and glory in the world to come. They shall have even here upon earth, hopes, and joys, and sensible comforts sufficient to make up for all that they lose. They shall find in the communion of saints, new friends, new relations, new companions, more loving, faithful, and valuable than any they had before their conversion. Their introduction into the family of God shall be an abundant recompense for exclusion from the society of this world. This may sound startling

Jesus and the
Man in the Tree

Luke 19:1–10

*Jesus said to him, "Today salvation has come to this house,
because this man, too, is a son of Abraham. For the Son of
Man came to seek and to save what was lost." (Luke 19:9–10)*

In the summer of 1929 a young Cambridge scholar knelt
down in the quiet of his room and prayed to God. In his
words, this act of prayer constituted "giving in" to a God
whose pursuit had been relentless, even unscrupulous. Prior
to that moment he had been a committed atheist, to all appearances immune to all forms of Christian witness. And
yet, C. S. Lewis tells us that all the while he was struggling
against the claims to God's existence. On all sides he was
confronted with challenges to his unbelief. "Really," he

writes, "a young Atheist cannot guard his faith too care-fully."[1]

> You must picture me alone in that room in Mag-dalen, night after night, feeling, whenever my mind lifted even for a second from my work, the steady, unrelenting approach of Him whom I so earnestly desired not to meet. That which I greatly feared had at last come upon me. In the Trinity Term of 1929 I gave in, and admitted that God was God, and knelt and prayed.[2]

The Man in the Tree

Lewis is not the only one who has encountered the "steady, unrelenting approach" of Jesus Christ. This passage in Luke 19 involves another man who gave no appearance of interest in God or susceptibility to the gospel, and yet Je-sus Christ was closing in on him with the same relentless treading. The encounter takes place in Jericho, and yet it might well have been Cambridge, where C. S. Lewis awaited God's coming, or even in your city or town, where those same footsteps are heard and felt.

This encounter comes to us in a brief ten verses that are easily organized into three phases: before Zacchaeus's meet-ing with Jesus, during that meeting, and then the aftermath and result of his fateful encounter with the Seeker and Sav-ior of the lost. Zacchaeus's story is that of the smallest act of faith producing the greatest change, all because it brought him to Jesus Christ. Here is how Luke tells us it began:

> Jesus entered Jericho and was passing through. A man was there by the name of Zacchaeus; he was a

chief tax collector and was wealthy. He wanted to see who Jesus was, but being a short man he could not, because of the crowd. So he ran ahead and climbed a sycamore-fig tree to see him, since Jesus was coming that way. (Luke 19:1–4)

In our studies of these encounters we are asking what brought Jesus and the various people together. This time the answer for Jesus is simple: he was passing through this city on his way to Jerusalem. He had an appointment up the road, one that he explained to his disciples just before these events:

Jesus took the Twelve aside and told them, "We are going up to Jerusalem, and everything that is written by the prophets about the Son of Man will be fulfilled. He will be handed over to the Gentiles. They will mock him, insult him, spit on him, flog him and kill him. On the third day he will rise again." (Luke 18:31–33)

That is what brought Jesus to Jericho. He was passing through, on his way to the cross.

What, then, about Zacchaeus? This brief description tells us quite a lot about him. First, he was a Jew; his name gives evidence to that. Second, he was not only a tax collector but also a chief tax collector. In our earlier study of Matthew's conversion, we saw how callous and hated the tax collectors inevitably were, working hand in hand with the occupying Romans to fleece the people. Zaccheus was not merely one of this number, but he was their chief in Jericho. Probably this means that he handled the bids with the Romans and supervised the actions of lesser publicans like Matthew had been. No wonder, then, that Luke tells us he was a very wealthy man.

Jericho was a significant and prosperous city, having been made into a little paradise by Herod the Great some years before. An indication of its wealth is that Mark Antony once had given it to his lover Cleopatra to show his affection. Jericho was the source of great revenue for the Romans, the hub of a vast trade network, so it was an important regional center. Imagine the tolls and tariffs and extortions that must have been collected by the tax officials. And over all of that sat this man Zacchaeus.

Few people, I am sure, would have guessed at his interest in a religious leader passing by, Jesus of Nazareth. Zacchaeus must always have had pressing business, important meetings, details to consider, and people to intimidate. Consumed in the world of money and power, few such men have time for or interest in spiritual matters. Yet we are told that "he wanted to see who Jesus was." He was interested in Jesus, so much so that when Zacchaeus failed to see through the crowds, being short of stature, "he ran ahead and climbed a sycamore-fig tree to see him, since Jesus was coming that way" (Luke 19:4).

Why was Zacchaeus looking for Jesus? Most of the commentators put it down to simple curiosity. Something of interest was breaking the dull routine. Jesus was now famous and was passing through, so it was natural to not want to miss the scene. Let me give you reasons, however, why I think far more was at work in the case of Zacchaeus than curiosity.

The first reason is that these actions suggest a meekness that is inconsistent with everything else we know about Zacchaeus. It seems that he lost himself at the thought of seeing Jesus. Everything he did here was hardly in keeping with the decorum of a tough boss like Zacchaeus must have been. Something was driving this man that even he may not have been aware of.

His running like a boy was inconsistent with the decorum of the great. He might instead have pushed his way forward into the crowd, let people know who he was, perhaps paid out some pittance from his riches to gain a good front-row seat. Were he merely curious, those are the actions that would have served a man such as him. Instead he raced to the sycamore tree, which was convenient because of its many low branches that he could climb into and for the cover its dense foliage provided. There Zacchaeus could step out of his role and look upon Jesus. His face could take on honest emotions; any look of wonder or joy would not be seen by others who would take it as a sign of weakness. Everything about his behavior suggests a meekness and vulnerability that could only be the result of spiritual working.

Second, all this suggests a stronger desire than what can be accounted for by curiosity. Suddenly, perhaps in a way surprising to himself, Zacchaeus was driven to set his eyes upon Jesus. Alfred Edersheim offers some reasonable conjectures:

> What had brought him? Certainly, not curiosity only. Was it the long working of conscience; or a dim, scarcely self-avowed hope of something better; or had he heard Him before; or of Him . . . that Jesus received—nay, called to Him the publicans and sinners? Or was it only the nameless, deep, irresistible inward drawing of the Holy Ghost?[3]

One thing we can be sure of is that Zacchaeus is not the only person who secretly is drawn to see Jesus. This is important for Christians to realize, that men and women we know who give no evidence of spiritual interest are often quite interested. They don't let us know, but they climb into their sycamore trees. They are thinking about God, they are concerned about a possible judgment, their conscience is working, they secretly wonder if there isn't more than just the things they know of in this life. Zacchaeus stands for a whole class of people, secret and unnoticed, who think far more seriously and more often about spiritual concerns than ever we will know.

How many of them would like the thing Zacchaeus sought? They want to see Jesus. They may be afraid to enter the church, they are afraid to read a Bible, they are reluctant to attend an explicitly religious meeting. But they are interested to see Jesus and to learn about him.

The other side to this coin is what Lewis called "the steady, unrelenting approach of God." There is grace at work unseen in the lives of men and women. "No one can come to me," said Jesus, "unless the Father who sent me draws him" (John 6:44). And the Father is drawing people, in ways large and small, open and subtle, relentlessly working in those he would save. We do not see it at the time, do not realize it until much later. But even now God is working in the lives of people like Zacchaeus. Despite every reason to write them off, as surely every religious person in Jericho must have written off Zacchaeus, we must be willing and eager to show them Jesus, leaving their salvation in his capable hands.

The Friend of Sinners

That leads us to the encounter between Jesus and Zacchaeus. Luke tells us, "When Jesus reached the spot, he

looked up and said to him, 'Zacchaeus, come down immediately. I must stay at your house today.' So he came down
at once and welcomed him gladly" (Luke 19:5–6).

What a surprise it must have been to Zacchaeus when
Jesus slowed and then came to a stop before his sycamore
tree. Those who were watching must have wondered if Jesus knew anything about this man he was favoring with attention. Their question was soon answered; Jesus knew
even his name. "Zacchaeus," he cried. How they, as well as
Zacchaeus, must have marveled at this knowledge. Perhaps,
then, Jesus was going to upbraid this scoundrel in front of
all the people. That would please the crowd—Jesus as a
populist politician. But that is not why he came. How stunning must have been his words that followed: "Zacchaeus,
come down immediately. I must stay at your house today."
The words had stunning significance for Zacchaeus, as for
the crowd: "I must stay at your house, Zacchaeus, today!"

At this point the crowd's rapt attention must have
transferred to the tax collector in the tree. What would he
do? Would he sneer at this religious simpleton? Would he
mock such fellowship in defiance? There are good reasons
for expecting that type of reaction from this kind of man.
What happened tells us much about Jesus' power and attractiveness: "He came down at once and welcomed him
gladly."

There are a number of things we might consider, beginning with the effectual call of Christ that produced such a
response in this hardened sinner. That is something we
studied earlier in Jesus' encounter with Matthew, at his tax
collector booth in Capernaum. Therefore I will allow
Matthew Henry's comment to suffice: "Christ invited himself to Zacchaeus' house. . . . He brings his own welcome;
he opens the heart and inclines it to receive him."[4]

Jesus not only opened Zacchaeus's heart with his power but also melted it with his kindness. How different was his attitude toward this sinner from that of everyone else in Jericho. A man like Zacchaeus might gain respect, surely fear, but these would have to dwell amidst the hatred and contempt the tax collectors received from the general populace. The one thing he surely was not prepared for was kindness, a warm offer of companionship, a genuine desire to spend time with him, to listen and get to know him, to enter into his house and into his life. That is what Jesus offered Zacchaeus, and its effect was powerfully obvious.

In the world of Jesus and Zacchaeus, sharing a meal was not a trivial exercise but a statement of personal acceptance and comradeship. This was more than a tax collector could dare to hope for. He had just wanted to see Jesus, to look at him with his own eyes. Now he would get to know him on a personal level, become a friend and comrade, to have fellowship with Jesus.

I do not want to discount the divine work of grace that produces every salvation experience, but imagine the effect this offer from Jesus must have had on a man like Zacchaeus. At this point he knew nothing of the cross or the empty tomb, both of which he later would come to understand, no doubt. What won him was Jesus' offer of personal fellowship even though he was a man of scandalous sin and evil reputation. Ignorant of Christianity, Zacchaeus accepted Christ, and through him came the faith that follows. That is the way it always is, and that is why it is Christ we must proclaim and share with people like Zacchaeus.

We forget how powerful this is, Christ's readiness to befriend those who come to him. How many people in this world, in our families, in our workplaces, have no one to befriend them, no one who would care to step across their threshold to spend time with them, to know them and be-come true friends. How much of the anger or meanness or bitter resentment people express is the result of their sense of rejection in a world that does not love like this.

It is therefore social pariahs like Zacchaeus who ought to be the specialty of the church in its outreach. If we want to be like Jesus, and if we want to reach the lost for his sake, then we will stop at the tree of Zacchaeus, as it were, and initiate a friendship that will often, we surely will find, lead to the salvation of even calloused sinners like him. J. C. Ryle is surely right to say, "Nothing is so frequently found to turn the hearts of great sinners, as the unexpected and undeserved tidings that Christ loves them and cares for their souls. These tidings have often broken and melted hearts of stone."[5]

Jesus' offer of friendship had an effect on this chief tax collector. Luke tells us, "So he came down at once and wel-comed him gladly." Surely there is some symbolism in this action. He who was high came down to be saved; he who was hidden among the leaves came out into the light to ac-cept Jesus' offer. Zacchaeus's eagerness is especially evident. He came down "at once." Though a chief among men, he was eager to obey when it was Jesus who called. "Come down at once," Jesus commanded him, "so he came down at once." In all of this, Zacchaeus is a model of a heart truly penetrated by the saving grace of Christ.

Salvation Proved in Repentance

It is uncertain how long Jesus stayed in Zacchaeus's house. Luke 19:7 says he became a guest, and the Greek term there may suggest taking up lodging. It is therefore conceivable that Jesus spent the night with Zacchaeus or

back four times the amount." This was not a mere pious statement but readiness to pay out money. He is grieved about his sins, the harm he has caused, and is eager to do something about it.

It is noteworthy that according to the law, money illegally acquired need only be repaid with a 20 percent penalty (see Lev. 6:1–5). Only rustlers of cattle or sheep were required to pay back four for one. Apparently, then, Zacchaeus pictures the worst kind of thief in all the law and puts himself in that category. He judges himself more sternly than God does. This intensity, along with his desire for tangible restitution, proves the reality of his change of heart.

Finally, his repentance is made complete by a changed attitude. It is often said that repentance means turning around, and that is true, but it also means walking forward in that new direction. That is exactly what we find in the case of Zacchaeus. "Here and now," he exclaims, "I give half of my possessions to the poor." Again, he exceeds the normal expectation, for the Israelites considered 20 percent the highest generosity that could be considered prudent. Zacchaeus, once the chief of swindlers, is overflowing with generosity. Once noted for the skill that served his greed, he now takes off to foolish excess of charity.

In that part of his life most dedicated to sin and to self—his treatment of money and of people—Zacchaeus not only repented but also became a model of grace. If you want to please Jesus, and if you want to vindicate his willingness to fellowship with you, then this is an excellent model. Have you been a drunk? Then take special joy in offering sobriety and moderation to Jesus Christ. Has your mouth been given to filth? Then make it a gift of love to Jesus, a special mark of his work in your life, to consecrate your lips to godly and uplifting speech. Have you been proud and brash and self-serving? Then make humility and gentle service for others an offering of love to please the Lord. That is what Zacchaeus did, and Jesus' delight is evident: Jesus said to him, "Today salvation has come to this house, because this man, too, is a son of Abraham."

Perhaps for all of his adult life, Zacchaeus had been a traitor to Israel. He had forfeited his birthright as a child of Abraham. Now in Christ, he finds his true identity. Surely Jesus meant these words for the ears of the crowd, as well as for the pleasure of his convert. The son of Abraham is not merely the one who talks of the Bible and boasts of a godly heritage but the one who turns to God with the faith that marked Abraham's life and here shows up in Zacchaeus.

Not long before this, Jesus had encountered another rich man, a man of virtue and high reputation who nonetheless was unable to do what Zacchaeus so gladly now proposed. When that rich young ruler turned away from Jesus, our Lord remarked, "How hard it is for the rich to enter the kingdom of God! Indeed, it is easier for a camel to go through the eye of a needle than for a rich man to enter the kingdom of God" (Luke 18:24–25). Here was that camel, a living testimony to the words of Christ: "What is impossible with men is possible with God" (v. 27).

To Seek and to Save

Our passage concludes with one of the great statements in all the New Testament. It is a statement that explains this encounter and the salvation of such a man as Zacchaeus: "For the Son of Man came to seek and to save what was lost" (Luke 19:10).

Here Jesus defines his whole purpose in the world. It

was for the lost that he came, and that is why he stopped before Zacchaeus's tree, surely the most lost man in all of Jericho that day. This tells us that no one is ineligible for salvation. We say that people are lost and it is for them that he came; therefore there is no one too lost to be found by Jesus. You are not too lost, and no one else you know is ineligible for the forgiveness of sins. There is no one of whom we should despair, because it is the lost he came to seek and to save. That is why Jesus came down this road, why he initiated this encounter: "The Son of Man came to seek and to save what was lost."

This one verse serves as the grand explanation for the whole of Christ's incarnation. The first verb explains what happened: He came. God has come to us. The second person of the Trinity left his glory in heaven and came into our world. That is the answer for those who want to know what God is doing about the mess of this world. He came; he entered our world.

Why, then, did he come? Why was the baby born in Bethlehem? Why did God's Son take on flesh and dwell among us? He came to seek and to save. If his purpose was to condemn us, he need not have come; we were already condemned. If his purpose was to rule or destroy, he would not have come in the weakness of our human nature. We find that everything he did, every word he said and every tear he shed, all the pain and sorrow of life that he embraced, all the unjust opposition of sinful men he endured, all the wrath of God he accepted in our place while he died upon the cross, all was for this: to seek and to save.

If you are a Christian, this is why you are saved. Not that you were seeking God but that Jesus was seeking you. Before he came into your life, before he found you hiding in your tree, he knew your name just as he knew Zacchaeus's. Before you ever gave thought to spiritual realities, he was thinking of you. He sought you and, having found you, he saved you by the power of his mighty grace.

If you are not a Christian, if you are reading this to catch a glimpse of Jesus passing by, or even for reasons you yourself can only vaguely guess, this message is especially for you. I mentioned earlier that C. S. Lewis said an unbeliever must guard his faith only too carefully, and perhaps you know something of this. The reason is that Jesus is seeking, his claims press upon you, your need of him grows more profound. Lewis described his conversion as "giving in" to God. That is what it is; you cease resisting his seeking of your heart. You cease rejecting his offer to love and to save you. Yes, you "give in" to Jesus. And yet, I don't think that is how Zacchaeus would put it at all. I think he would sing in the words of the hymn:

Amazing grace!—how sweet the sound—
   that saved a wretch like me!
I once was lost, but now am found,
   was blind, but now I see.

Perhaps you are held back because you realize that what happened to Zacchaeus may happen to you if you, too, accept Jesus. He gave away his treasured riches, and you fear to lose your treasured sins and possessions. Let me observe, then, that Zacchaeus would hardly have called this loss. This is a story not of loss but of gain, great gain. What he saw in Jesus made him forget his money, allowed him to think of everything in a new and different and joyful light. Yes, that will happen to you if you open your heart to Jesus. Zacchaeus's soul had not been satisfied, or he would not have climbed that tree. Something was missing, something was lost, so he went seeking it, to find it in the face of Christ.

The same is true for you. You are seeking joy, you are seeking peace, you are seeking rest and hope and meaning. And in all of these Jesus Christ is seeking you. If you will look to him, you will find what you were searching for, even eternal life. You who were lost will be found by the One who came to seek and to save you.

Jesus and the Governor

John 18:28–19:16

Jesus said, "My kingdom is not of this world. If it were, my servants would fight to prevent my arrest by the Jews. But now my kingdom is from another place." "You are a king, then!" said Pilate. (John 18:36–37)

In his monumental work, *City of God*, Augustine states that there are two cities, the City of Man and the City of God. He writes:

> Two societies have issued from two kinds of love. Worldly society has flowered from a selfish love which dared to despise even God, whereas the communion of saints is rooted in a love of God that is

ready to trample on self. In a word, this latter relies on the Lord, whereas the other boasts that it can get along by itself. The city of man seeks the praise of men, whereas the height of glory for the other is to hear God in the witness of conscience. The one lifts up its head in its own boasting; the other says to God: "Thou art my glory, thou liftest up my head" (Ps. 3:4).[1]

Augustine's ideas are important for Christians today, because we are still faced with these two cities or realms. We are part of the city of this world and the City of God; we must render unto Caesar what belongs to him and to God what belongs to God.

In the Bible, these two cities are mainly described as two kingdoms, that of heaven and that of the world, and I do not think there is any more telling interaction between them than in the passage from John that we will study in this chapter. This is, in many respects, a different kind of encounter from those we have looked at earlier. In all our previous studies on encounters with Jesus, our Lord was the one in control. It was others who came before him; he was the one who dictated the course and the outcome. Now we find our Lord Jesus brought before the worldly powers as represented by Pontius Pilate, the Roman governor of Judea. Jesus stands before Pilate, and Pilate decides what his fate will be.

This is an important and lengthy passage, and I do not propose to cover everything that is found in it. In particular, I will not discuss in detail the relationship between church and state, about which this passage speaks with great significance. What I want to focus on is the encounter between Jesus and Pilate, which is an encounter between two kingdoms, between two value systems, and between two judgments.

Two Different Kingdoms

The passage begins as Jesus is led by the Jewish leaders to Pilate's residence in Jerusalem, after his arrest the night before. Earlier in the morning the Jewish trial had taken place, with Jesus falsely accused of various crimes. When that failed, they asked him directly if he was the Christ and Son of God. Jesus admitted that he was, and on that basis alone they convicted him of blasphemy (Mark 14:61–63). That presented a problem to the Jewish leaders, because the punishment for this was death, but they did not have the authority to carry out the sentence. The Romans had reserved for themselves the right to execute capital punishment, so Jesus had to be brought to the governor to be convicted by him.

We know quite a lot about Pontius Pilate, from the Bible and from other historical sources. All of the evidence points to him as a man who was simultaneously brutal and morally weak. Appointed governor of Judea by Tiberius Caesar in A.D. 26, he held that post until A.D. 37. Pilate's tactless policies often spurred public outrage and revolt, which he then savagely suppressed.

How fitting he was, then, to represent the kingdom of this world as it encounters the kingdom of God in the person of Jesus Christ. Pilate shows us what gives the worldly kingdom its power. Pilate relied on the force of arms, by virtue of the legions of Rome. These soldiers required support, and so Pilate also relied on taxes. Worldly princes always rule by means of these things, along with pomp and ceremony, prestige, and alliances with other rulers. Modern governments have expanded this list to include manipulation of the press and propaganda, along with technological, scientific, and economic prowess. It is with such resources that the kingdom of the world exerts its rule, and we have to say that it is all quite impressive. Pilate's rule over the Jews was close to absolute; we see this vividly portrayed as the religious leaders had to bring Jesus to him for disposition.

It seems clear that the Jews were hoping for a quick acceptance of their verdict, followed by Jesus' swift execution. Pilate, however, probably toying with them, did not go along so easily. He came out to them and asked, "What charges are you bringing against this man?" (John 18:29). That statement signaled that a real trial was going to take place, since the declaration of charges was the first step in the Roman legal procedure. " 'If he were not a criminal,' they replied, 'we would not have handed him over to you'" (v. 30). Pilate did not go along with them, telling them instead to deal with the matter themselves, to which they tellingly responded, "But we have no right to execute anyone" (v. 31). The Old Testament law did give the Jews the right of capital punishment, a right the Romans has taken away. John tells us that in this God was at work, ensuring that Jesus would die in the manner foretold, by the method of crucifixion, which only the Romans employed: "This happened so that the words Jesus had spoken indicating the kind of death he was going to die would be fulfilled" (v. 32).

At this point Pilate returned to Jesus, who was inside, and asked him, "Are you the king of the Jews?" (v. 33). The other Gospels tell us that this was a specific charge the Jews had made against Jesus, and Pilate pursues the matter directly, proceeding to the investigation of the case. Jesus answered, with words that sound evasive: "Is that your own idea, or did others talk to you about me?" (v. 34).

This is not evasion, however, but an important point Jesus needed to make. What Jesus queried was the perspective from which Pilate was asking the question. Was he confronting Jesus on the charge of setting up a worldly kingdom opposed to that of Caesar? In that sense the answer would be no, for Jesus was not a rival to Pilate in Judea. But if the question was coming from the Jewish perspective, the answer must be yes. Jesus was the Messiah, the long-awaited king from the line of David.

Pilate's answer follows this line of reasoning. "Am I a Jew?" he asks. He had no interest in purely ethnic or religious matters but only those that affected the sovereign rights of Caesar and his kingdom. It is in that sense that Pilate wanted to know, "What is it you have done?"

This exchange sets the stage for an important statement regarding Christ and his kingdom. Jesus explains his position to Pilate by saying, "My kingdom is not of this world. If it were, my servants would fight to prevent my arrest by the Jews. But now my kingdom is from another place" (John 18:36).

This statement tells us two vital things about Christ's kingdom, beginning with the words "my kingdom." The point is that Jesus Christ is a king. This man, standing as a prisoner before the worldly governor, brought in as a criminal by the world, bearing no symbols or accouterments of worldly power, is a king. The audacity of this claim was not lost on Pilate. In John 18:33, when he first questioned Jesus, he emphasized the contrast between the idea of his kingship and his lowly appearance. In the Greek text a clear emphasis is placed on the pronoun *you*. "You," he says, "are you a king?"

That is a way of thinking that is not restricted to Pontius Pilate. People think the same way today. Oh, Jesus might be a worthy fellow, a nice example in a spiritual sort of way, but he is not a power to be reckoned with. Everything about him makes that plain. Jesus commands no armies; he does not decide who gets promoted, who becomes rich, who rises in rank in the world. He may be a nice religious model, but he is not someone to take too seriously.

Yet Jesus insists that he is a king, that he has a kingdom. But it is not a kingdom like any other in the world. "My kingdom," he explains, "is not of this world." Jesus' kingdom is a spiritual one. It is not like the kingdom Pilate represents. If his kingdom is not of this world, then it must be of some other origin, and that origin is heaven. Jesus reigns with spiritual and with heavenly authority. That means that it is over the soul that Jesus reigns, through spiritual power and heavenly principles. As the hymn puts it:

> For not with swords loud clashing,
>   nor roll of stirring drums,
> but deeds of love and mercy,
>   the heav'nly kingdom comes.

Let me ask, then: Does this mean that while you must respect earthly powers, you can afford to ignore Jesus' kingdom? If Jesus' rule is merely spiritual, does that mean it has nothing to do with people who don't choose to be religious? James Montgomery Boice answers this in his commentary on John, writing:

> Nothing is farther from the truth, for when we say that Christ's kingdom is not of this world, what we are really saying is that Christ's kingdom is of heaven and therefore has an even greater claim over us than do the earthly kingdoms we know so

well. . . . Over these is Christ, and we flout His kingship not merely at the peril of our fortune and lives
but at the peril of our eternal souls.[2]

As Jesus put it, "Do not be afraid of those who kill the
body but cannot kill the soul. Rather, be afraid of the One
who can destroy both soul and body in hell" (Matt. 10:28).
Despite appearances, Jesus claims a kingship that is far
more ominous and significant than any other power in the
world.

The Values of This World

This encounter is not only between two kingdoms and
the different powers they represent but also between two
radically different value systems. In the actions of Pilate
and the Jewish leaders we see the values of the kingdom of
this world.

The first of these is utilitarianism, or what we might call
pragmatism. Our world believes in and practices whatever
works. That is the religion of mankind, and especially of
America. This value is clearly present in this encounter between Pilate and Jesus.

We see this in the behavior of the Jews. Things were
not going well for them that morning. First, rather than
rubber stamping their condemnation, Pilate demanded a
charge. John does not give us the Jewish leaders' full reply,
but we find it in other Gospels: "We have found this man
subverting our nation. He opposes payment of taxes to Caesar and claims to be Christ, a king" (Luke 23:2). Two of
those claims were outright lies. Jesus had done nothing to
subvert the nation of Israel, and attempts to establish that
with false witnesses during the Jewish trial broke down be-

cause of contradictions. With regard to paying taxes to Caesar, their earlier attempt to trap Jesus on this matter had failed miserably. When asked if it was lawful to pay taxes to Caesar, Jesus held up a coin with Caesar's inscription upon it and gave the famous answer that says so much about church and state relations: "Give to Caesar what is Caesar's, and to God what is God's" (Luke 20:25). Why did the Jews make these false charges? Because they thought it expedient to lie; they thought that it would work. Because they were pragmatists.

It did not work, however, for as John 18:38 tells us, Pilate acquitted Jesus of the charges against him. "I find no basis for a charge against him." That was the formal ruling of this formal court of law. At that point the Jews changed their complaint. In John 19:7 they gave their most honest charge, "We have a law, and according to that law he must die, because he claimed to be the Son of God." But that was no concern to Pilate, who cared nothing for theological disputes, so the Jewish leaders changed their approach once again. We see this in John 19:12, "The Jews kept shouting, 'If you let this man go, you are no friend of Caesar. Anyone who claims to be a king opposes Caesar.'" Now we have a wholesale abandonment of any pretense to justice, in favor of direct intimidation. If Pilate did not go along with condemning Jesus, they would use it to discredit him with Caesar in Rome, something that had proven fatal in the case of many other officials. In summary, the Jewish leaders threw justice and truth aside, operating by pure expediency, which is the way of this world.

We find the same value governing Pilate's actions. Initially he conducted the trial with great care and even propriety. He would not let Jesus be condemned without formal charges and a real trial. It is not clear why he acted so out of character in this manner, but the best suggestion seems to have to do with a message he received from his wife. Matthew 27:19 tells us, "While Pilate was sitting on the judge's seat, his wife sent him this message: 'Don't have anything to do with that innocent man, for I have suffered a great deal today in a dream because of him.'"

In any case, Pilate began these procedures in keeping with the Roman tradition of law and justice. But when the pressure against him began to mount he too responded with blatant expediency. In John 18:38 he declared Jesus innocent, but instead of releasing him as he should, Pilate turned to a custom apparently then in practice of granting one free pardon in recognition of the annual Passover. Matthew's Gospel makes it especially clear that Pilate gave the people the choice between Jesus and a man named Barabbas, a notorious insurrectionist. "Which one do you want me to release to you," he said, "Barabbas, or Jesus who is called Christ?" (Matt. 27:17). "Give us Barabbas!" they cried, and therefore Pilate held onto Jesus.

At this point Pilate committed another great injustice, again out of his commitment to pure expediency. John 19 begins by telling us:

> Then Pilate took Jesus and had him flogged. The soldiers twisted together a crown of thorns and put it on his head. They clothed him in a purple robe and went up to him again and again, saying, "Hail, king of the Jews!" And they struck him in the face. Once more Pilate came out and said to the Jews, "Look, I am bringing him out to you to let you know that I find no basis for a charge against him." When Jesus came out wearing the crown of thorns and the purple robe, Pilate said to them, "Here is the man!" (vv. 1–5)

the latter as its ally. The two go together in the postmodern twenty-first century just as they did in the pagan first century. Self-serving pragmatists cannot afford the idea of absolute truth. Truth is an encumbrance if our highest aim is to serve our self-chosen good. This is what lay behind the scorn of Pontius Pilate, a man whose power rested on the sword. To the kingdom of this world truth is nothing; from the lips of those who serve nothing higher than personal ambition we will ever hear the words of Pilate, "What is truth?"

Let me briefly observe what these two values produce, in the time of Jesus and now. They produce hypocrisy, injustice, and cruelty. Look at the Jewish leaders: could there be a more hypocritical sight? They are eager to hand over the sinless Son of God; they come with trumped-up charges and false testimony, without a moment's hesitation. And yet they are careful to stay outside the precincts of Pilate's house, lest they should be defiled for the Passover. What a picture they are of the hypocrisy of this world! The same may be said of Pilate's whole show of supposed justice. It was, at bottom, one great sham, just as hypocrisy is found in every corner of the kingdom of this world.

The second result of the world's value system is injustice. With everyone out for themselves or at least their interest group, with everyone treating truth as something to be manipulated, it is impossible that justice should ever prevail.

The injustices in this trial are rife. First there is the bringing of Jesus; his treatment by the Jews was an enormity of injustice and lies. Pilate, for all his procedural correctness, is hardly any better. In John 19:4 he formally acquits our Lord but then has him savagely beaten. In the end, faced with the slightest threat to his personal well-being, he ends with words that condemn the justice of the kingdom represented by him: "Finally Pilate handed him over to them to be crucified" (John 19:16).

Last, under the reign of this kingdom and its values, ours is a cold and cruel world. "Behold the man," cried the hypocritical and unjust governor, to a crowd worthy of the same description. There stood Jesus Christ, the righteous One, the Good Shepherd, the healer, and the teacher sent from God, now bloodied and brutally abused, clothed in mock regalia, crowned with thorns that tore the flesh around his brow. How chilling it is that all this cruel display was an attempt at mercy on the part of Pilate. And yet even so pitiful a sight as this left the Jewish leaders unmoved. Such was their cruelty that they only replied, "Crucify! Crucify!" Martyn Lloyd-Jones observes:

> If you want to know what this world is like, look what it did to him. . . . He gave himself to healing people, and to instructing them. He never did anyone any harm. He went about doing good. What was the response of the world? It hated him, it persecuted him, it rejected him. It chose a murderer before him. It crucified him, it killed him.[3]

"Behold the man," Pilate cried. It was a man he had declared innocent. It was the man sent from heaven to bring a kingdom from above. Here was the man of all men, and if Pilate meant by his words to strip Jesus of his dignity, how miserably he failed.

The Reign of Truth

The man Pilate set forth was a king, but a king as different from Pilate as the two were in appearance. What shall we say about Christ's kingdom but that it is everything the kingdom of this world is not; and everything that is of the world is not of Christ. That is why utilitarian pragmatism and relativism in truth or morals are always the worst things for Christians to fall into. To embrace these is to fall prey to the kingdom of this world. "Do not love the world or any-thing in the world," writes the apostle John. "For everything in the world . . . comes not from the Father but from the world. The world and its desires pass away, but the man who does the will of God lives forever" (1 John 2:15–17).

Christ's reign is not of these, but as he says, it is a reign of truth. "For this reason I was born," says our Lord, "and for this I came into the world, to testify to the truth. Everyone on the side of truth listens to me" (John 18:37).

For Jesus and his kingdom, truth is not something to be twisted or manipulated but to be revealed. "I came to reveal the truth," he says. Surely we see the reality of this as Jesus allows himself to be falsely charged, brutally abused, and tortuously crucified. Why? To do the work of his kingdom, to reveal the truth.

Obviously, then, the truth his kingdom stands upon is not like that of the world. This is not the truth of pragma-tism, which is never willing to die; it is not the truth of rel-ativism, which has nothing to die for. Jesus has the truth because he is truth. He is the great reality that shapes all things, the Word that became flesh and dwelt among us (John 1:14). His truth, therefore, is not constructed; it is not discovered, partially and tentatively like some new theory of men. It is the truth that always was and is and will be, the truth he brings into the world from God and reveals as light into darkness.

I am reminded of a story told by James Montgomery Boice, my late pastor and colleague. He was on a plane,

and the woman seated next to him learned he was a
Christian minister. She began to bring out all her objec-
tions about Christianity. First she spoke of original sin,
how it made no sense and how she would not accept it.
Dr. Boice replied, "I see, but is it true?" Next she went on
to the idea of judgment and hell, how uncivilized and
amoral all of it was. "I see how you feel, but is it true?" he
replied. She went on to the next topic and then the next,
each with the same response. Finally she erupted with her
great distaste for everything taught in the Bible, how it
wasn't modern or appealing to her way of thinking. As
Dr. Boice began to open his mouth one last time, she exclaimed, "Oh, I know, I know, none of that matters. 'Is it
true?' you are going to say!"

That is what we need to say. It is truth that Christians
have to offer, truth we must be willing to stake our lives
upon. Particularly in a relativistic age, this is what the
world needs us to do, what a starving world is hungering for:
Truth we believe because it is true, because it is of God,
rather than merely because it is useful or palatable to us.
Therefore we should never seek popularity or measure success in worldly terms. When Christians have done that, we
have always rendered ourselves irrelevant. As members of
Christ's kingdom, as his disciples in this world, we must
take our stand upon the truth that is our greatest source of
power in this world; we must measure our success in terms
of faithfulness to the truth he has given us in the Bible. The
apostle Paul writes,

> The weapons we fight with are not the weapons of
> the world. On the contrary, they have divine
> power to demolish strongholds. We demolish ar-
> guments and every pretension that sets itself up

against the knowledge of God, and we take captive every thought to make it obedient to Christ.
(2 Cor. 10:4–5)

I have a Bible given me by a friend when I prepared to
enter seminary. In it he wrote: "Know the truth. Live the
truth. Tell the truth." That is about the best advice any
Christian can receive, especially one entering the ministry.
Above all of this, my friend wrote in that Bible, "He is
truth." That is what Jesus' kingdom is all about, Jesus who
is "the way and the truth and the life" (John 14:6). "Sanc-
tify them by the truth," he prayed to the Father; "your word
is truth." To us Jesus said, "If you hold to my teaching, you
are really my disciples. Then you will know the truth, and
the truth will set you free" (John 8:31–32).

Two Judgments

We have seen here two kingdoms and two value systems, and I want to conclude by observing that there are
also two judgments in this scene. Only one of them is obvious, the one decreed by the kingdom of the world, by
Pontius Pilate the governor. John 19:16 says, "Pilate
handed him over to them to be crucified."

I said in the beginning that this encounter differs from
the others in that Jesus stands before Pilate, because Pilate
judges Christ. But that really wasn't the case. If one thing
comes through in this account, it is that Jesus was in control, despite being a prisoner in Pilate's court. Pilate was not
the judge, nor were the leaders of the Jews. Instead they
were the ones on trial. It is the same today. Man wants to
put God on the stand, while man sits on the judge's bench.
But all the while the situation is reversed.

Pilate condemned himself when he acknowledged that Jesus was innocent of all crime and then handed him over for execution. Even worse is the case of the Jewish leaders. Stunningly, when faced with Jesus, the king of the Davidic line and the Messiah of God, they sealed their condemnation with these terrible words: "We have no king but Caesar" (John 19:15). Because of this, their rejection of the true king God had sent, God abandoned the Jews to their Roman rulers. In a few short decades Caesar would tear down the walls of Jerusalem. History records that these words have had the most dreadful of implications for the Jewish people. In a way more ultimate than ever before they had betrayed and rejected their God, only to be rejected by him in return.

All this comes into focus in John 19:10, where Pilate said to Jesus, "Don't you realize I have power either to free you or to crucify you?" "I have power," said Pilate, and he did. But Jesus replied, "You would have no power over me if it were not given to you from above. Therefore the one who handed me over to you is guilty of a greater sin" (v. 11). So it is. The kingdom of this world has power, power that comes from God, but this world and its kingdom will yet be judged by God. Far from exonerating Pilate, simply because the guilt of the Jews was greater, Jesus affirms God's judgment over Pilate and over all.

By Pilate's decree, Jesus Christ was crucified, dead, and buried. We affirm this weekly through our creed in the church. But God, who overrules the judgment of this world, raised him from the dead to everlasting life and seated him at the right hand of his majesty in heaven. That is what Peter preached to these same men just weeks later, in his great Pentecost sermon: "You, with the help of wicked men, put him to death by nailing him to the cross. But God raised him from the dead, freeing him from the agony of death" (Acts 2:23–25). Such was the judgment of God in the case of Jesus Christ, overruling the governor's decree.

There is no one to overrule God's judgment, and every one of us will face it. "Man is destined once to die, and after that to face judgment" (Heb. 9:27), says the Bible. The terms of that judgment are set forth in John 3:18, in terms of faith in Jesus Christ: "Whoever believes in him is not condemned, but whoever does not believe stands condemned already because he has not believed in the name of God's one and only Son."

"Everyone on the side of truth listens to me" (John 18:37), said Jesus to the governor. Those who hold to his teaching, to his truth, are saved by him. All those who reject the truth in this life will be exposed by the truth in the judgment to come. On the last day every sin will be exposed before the light of God's justice, and only those cleansed by the saving blood of Christ will be set free.

Jesus Christ sat judged by Pilate, the governor from Rome. But in the end those roles will be reversed. Pilate brought forth Jesus, battered and bruised. "Behold the man," he cried in derision. But the day will come when God will also set Jesus forth, crowned with glory and honor. He too will declare, "Behold the man." Then, as Paul writes in Philippians,

> . . . every knee should bow,
> in heaven and on earth and under the earth,
> and every tongue confess that Jesus Christ is Lord,
> to the glory of God the Father. (Phil. 2:10–11)

Jesus and the
Thief on the Cross

Luke 23:32–43

But the other criminal rebuked him. "Don't you fear God," he said, "since you are under the same sentence? We are punished justly, for we are getting what our deeds deserve. But this man has done nothing wrong." Then he said, "Jesus, remember me when you come into your kingdom." Jesus answered him, "I tell you the truth, today you will be with me in paradise." (Luke 23:40–43)

It should come as no surprise that the most important day in human history, the day Jesus Christ was crucified, was also the day when the greatest number of prophecies were fulfilled. In this short passage we find a great number of biblical predictions dramatically played out in great detail.

There were at least fifteen specific prophecies fulfilled in Christ's death. Among them was Isaiah 53:12, written more than seven hundred years beforehand, which says he "was numbered with the transgressors. For he bore the sin of many, and made intercession for the transgressors." Our passage shows the literal fulfillment of both of these statements. Psalm 22:18, given through King David in the tenth century B.C., says,

> They divide my garments among them
> and cast lots for my clothing.

We find that very thing in Luke's account of Jesus' death on the cross. Psalm 22:7–8 describes the mocking from the crowd with startling precision. Christ's death was sealed by the greatest fulfillments of prophecy ever.

Another way we might view these verses in Luke 23 is to see Jesus in his threefold office as prophet, priest, and king. Going back to Luke 23:28, we read of him prophesying to a group of weeping women about the judgment to come. In Luke 23:34, he makes intercession as priest for the people who then were crucifying him. Finally, in his dealing with the thief on the cross we see Jesus in his kingly office, reigning over and making provision for a subject of his heavenly realm.

My purpose in this chapter is to examine this account as an encounter between Jesus and the convicted criminal who was crucified next to him. Jesus had said, "The Son of Man came to seek and to save what was lost" (Luke 19:10). We find him doing that even in the darkest and most difficult circumstances Jesus possibly could face. In this encounter there are four important things for us to observe: first, an unlikely believer; second, a model profession; third, a ready Savior; and fourth, a complete salvation.

An Unlikely Believer

As this passage begins it does not seem likely that someone is about to receive salvation by coming to faith in Christ. Everyone here has come to either kill or mock or torment our Lord. And yet, even in a situation like this, there is going to be a salvation because the Savior is there.

Surely the more likely candidates for faith would be the Jews who watched this horrid crucifixion. These were the people for whom Jesus came in the most special sense, the people of the Old Testament, which pointed forward to him. It is only natural to assume that they would rally to his cause, but the opposite happened. Luke records their hateful derision, which so chillingly fulfills the prophecy of Psalm 22:7–8: "He saved others," they cried. "Let him save himself if he is the Christ of God, the Chosen One" (Luke 23:35). The Jews who most of all should have turned to Jesus in faith instead turned against him in cruel betrayal.

I suppose that makes the soldiers the next likely candidates. Soldiers are generally a rough breed, but they are often deeply spiritual men, as two different believing centurions demonstrate in Scripture. Soldiers are exposed to suffering and therefore more readily admit their need of a savior. They also face the reality and often the imminent prospect of death. None of that, however, softened the hearts of these Roman soldiers, who heartlessly abused Jesus that day. Luke 23:37 tells us they derided him as a supposed king. "If you are the king of the Jews," they mocked, "save yourself"—little aware of the legions of angels held back by Christ's willingness to suffer and die.

That leaves the criminals crucified with Jesus. These two had come involuntarily. Pilate no doubt arranged for them to be there to make a contemptuous statement to go with the sign he had placed over the cross. The sign said, "This is the King of the Jews" (Luke 23:38). Even from a biblical perspective the thieves seem to be there mainly as props to uphold the theme of Christ's fellowship with sinners. These criminals were not likely candidates for faith in Christ, as their criminal status argues. Mark's account bears out that assessment, telling us, "Those crucified with him also heaped insults on him" (Mark 15:32).

If you consider the verbs in these verses, you hear a steady drumbeat of scorn and rejection of Christ. The soldiers "led him out to be executed" (Luke 23:32). The people and rulers "sneered at him" (v. 35). They "mocked him" (v. 36). In Luke 23:39, the hanging thieves join the act: "One of the criminals who hung there hurled insults at him: 'Aren't you the Christ? Save yourself and us!' "

But at this point something remarkable happened. The other thief, who initially had been willing to join this abuse against Jesus, suddenly spoke out to rebuke his fellow criminal: "Don't you fear God, since you are under the same sentence? . . . This man has done nothing wrong" (vv. 40–41). His was an unlikely action, yet it is the kind of thing that Christianity's whole history consists of. In a world where Christ is despised, where Jesus hangs in weakness and derision, where all the voices around can only disparage the idea that he would be King and Lord and Savior, out cries one who sees in him beauty and righteousness and hope for salvation. "Jesus," he implored, "remember me when you come into your kingdom" (v. 42). It is that kind of unlikely faith that brings salvation to everyone who believes.

A Model Profession

If we narrow our focus to Jesus and the thieves, if we lift our eyes from the ground and only look on those hanging against the sky, what we find is a summary representation of all mankind. There are two men, one on each side of Jesus Christ. Both of them are guilty, both of them are condemned, both are about to feel the punishment of death. That is what they have in common, the great unifying factors of all mankind. There is only one significant difference between the two, and that is their attitude to Jesus Christ. One man rejects him, and one embraces him as Savior, confessing his sin and pleading for mercy.

That is the division created in this world by the cross of Christ, which stands between these two basic humanities. With one on Jesus' right and the other on Jesus' left, we have a dress rehearsal for the end of days. I find myself assuming that the believing thief was on Jesus' right, because in the judgment to come that is where the redeemed will be who enter into life. Then, as Jesus said in Matthew 25:41, "He will say to those on his left, 'Depart from me, you who are cursed, into the eternal fire prepared for the devil and his angels.'" To those on his right he will say, "Come, you who are blessed by my Father; take your inheritance, the kingdom prepared for you since the creation of the world" (Matt. 25:34).

This one thief's faith resulted in his salvation, and over the centuries his words have no doubt encouraged the faith of many others. There is scarcely a more encouraging example in all of Scripture of the power of simple faith to procure a complete and instantaneous salvation. In fact, this dying thief, hanging next to Jesus, presents to us a model profession of faith. Anyone who wonders what it means, what it would take, to have faith in Jesus and thus to be saved, has here a clear example to follow.

He begins with a reproof to his fellow thief. "Don't you fear God?" he demands (Luke 23:40). In the Greek it is a bit stronger: "Do not even you fear God?" Obviously he has in mind the impending death that will usher him and his colleague into the judgment of God. Realizing that he was about to die had a clarifying effect on his mind, and he marvels that it has not done the same for his colleague. Hebrews 9:27 says, "Man is destined to die once, and after that to face judgment." That is a reality that surely should sober up the most careless thinker.

The point is that faith in Christ begins with the fear of God and his coming judgment of sinners. These thieves were not the only ones faced with that reality; as I said earlier, in this they represent every member of the sinful human race. Unless you awake to the impending doom of God's wrath upon your sins, you too will be judged. Without the fear of God, you will never seriously turn to Jesus in faith but will go on treating him with boredom or contempt.

Second, this believing thief confessed himself a guilty sinner. Donald Grey Barnhouse explains the importance of this:

> This must be the position of anyone who is going to be saved. As long as we cling to our own selves and think that there is even a shred of righteousness in ourselves that could satisfy the demands of a holy God, there is no possibility of salvation for us. But when we recognize that we have sinned . . . then we are in the position of those who may obtain mercy.[1]

First is the fear of God, followed by a confession of sin. Next this man realized that Jesus is innocent of all wrong: "We are punished justly, for we are getting what our deeds deserve. But this man has done nothing wrong" (Luke 23:41). In light of the charges against Jesus, this surely means the thief believed Jesus was who he said he was. This is necessary in the salvation of every sinner. We must take our eyes off our guilty selves and look to Jesus as a righteous Savior. "Behold the Lamb of God," said John the Baptist, and we must if we are to be saved.

As this thief lifted his weary eyes to Jesus, our Lord was performing the work of our salvation before him. Jesus, the spotless sacrifice, was bearing the weight of sin in our place, taking to himself the just punishment for our transgressions. That was the work only a sinless Savior could do, the work for which he came, as he put it, "to give his life a ransom for many" (Matt. 20:28).

At this point, however, the thief is not yet saved, any more than you are saved if your faith is merely perceptive and intellectual. He sees the reality of life after death and of God's judgment—these are pressed upon him by his circumstances. Then he reflects upon his guilt and unworthiness. Although he had begun to join the mocking of Jesus, now he sees Christ's innocence—perhaps by his demeanor on the cross. All this leads him to take the fourth step that saves his soul: "Jesus," he said, "remember me when you come into your kingdom."

How remarkable that statement was. He alone in all this crowd addresses our Lord as he is dying, and he rightly uses the name that states his office. Before his birth, the angel had said to Joseph, "You are to give him the name Jesus, because he will save his people from their sins" (Matt. 1:21). It is only when we too turn to Jesus for a personal salvation, asking that he would not merely be a Savior in abstract but our Savior, my Savior—only then does salvation come upon a sinner's soul. For you, if you are not yet saved, this means praying to Jesus, confessing to him your sin, adoring his righteousness, and asking him who died next to this thief to apply that same saving work to your account.

This thief was saved when he turned to Jesus as One who wields authority over the eternity of souls. "Remember me when you come into your kingdom," he pleaded. He alone read the sign over Jesus' cross and recognized how true it was, that Jesus was king, not over a kingdom of this world but of the kingdom of heaven, king of the spiritual realm in which eternal destinies are judged.

Remember that this man was looking at Jesus not in his power as he cast out demons or healed the multitudes but in the moment of his greatest weakness and degradation. Jesus was dying with a couple of criminals, wracked with pain, derided by those who watched. Through all of this, this dying thief saw enough to grasp what the hymnist says of Jesus:

> Thou art the King of Israel,
>   thou David's royal Son,
> who in the Lord's name comest,
>   the King and blessed One!

Alexander Maclaren reflects upon the irony of this mockery Jesus endured. Speaking of the crown of thorns and the written notice on the cross, he writes:

> They crowned Him with thorns. . . . That mockery was a symbol which they who did it little dreamed of. The crown of thorns proclaims a sovereignty founded on sufferings. . . . The Cross leads to the crown.[2]

Therefore, when we see a cross we should think not merely of the defeat Jesus accepted for us, the death he endured, and the scorn he received. We must also see what this dying thief beheld, namely, his triumph over sin and death, the eternal life that conquered the grave, and the crown of glory of his sovereign and eternal reign.

These were the steps to this man's faith in Christ: the fear of God, the confession of sin, the glimpse of Jesus as sinless Savior, and the plea for personal salvation into the kingdom of God. Let me add that there is considerable evidence that this man's faith was genuine. Many people make expressions of faith when frightened, especially before death, and yet how few of these prove to be credible or last after the fear is gone. But this man backed up his profession of faith by his willingness to speak out for Jesus against the crowd. True Christian faith is always willing to identify with Jesus and share his reproach in the world.

A Ready Savior

That leads to our third point, a portrait of Jesus as a ready Savior. In all the great scenes of his life painted in words in the Gospels, I think there is none that more vividly makes this point, that Jesus is ready and eager to save every sinner who comes to him in faith.

Consider that if there was any time in all his life when we would expect Jesus to think about himself instead of others, then this had to be it. If Jesus had cried out with curses against these wretched hypocrites, these cruel and blasphemous people, this unjust world that hated him, who among us could complain? We are reckoning with Jesus at the moment of his greatest weakness, in his absolute lowest point, in his most despicable degradation, and look how ready he is to save the sinner!

We first encounter this marvel in Luke 23:34. Luke is sparse in his details; he brushes over the horror of what was happening to Jesus as they nailed his hands and feet and then slammed the cross into its mount, every blow pulsing through his flesh. What Luke wants to make sure we know is Jesus' reaction to all this, which is amazing and marvelous: "Jesus said, 'Father, forgive them, for they do not know what they are doing'" (v. 34).

Their ignorance was a culpable one; while ignorance mitigated their crime, it removed not one shred of the guilt. The point for us is Jesus' attitude toward these men who were even then gloating over his torment: it was an attitude of mercy and forgiveness. If Jesus is so eager for them to be saved, how must he look upon us, sinners though we are.

Speaking of their ignorance, what is Jesus doing but searching out the ground of hope for their souls? These are men who still can be persuaded by grace, and we find in the Book of Acts that many of them ultimately believed and were saved, surely in direct answer to this amazing prayer of grace. Who among us can fear to approach a Savior like this? No matter what you are, no matter what you have done to him, no matter your past record of sin, who can deny that Jesus is ready to accept you if only you will repent and believe on him?

After his resurrection, Jesus told his disciples to begin preaching salvation in this city, the city that had betrayed and killed him, and many of these people were saved. Peter, in one of his sermons in Jerusalem, pleaded with them in words that surely came from our Lord:

> Now, brothers, I know that you acted in ignorance, as did your leaders. But this is how God fulfilled

what he had foretold through all the prophets, saying that his Christ would suffer. Repent, then, and
turn to God, so that your sins may be wiped out,
that times of refreshing may come from the Lord.
(Acts 3:17–19)

That is the kind of Savior who sends his gospel out to
you, even now as his Word is preached. It is for your salvation, for the forgiveness of your sins, that he maintains this
testimony in the world. What possibly could keep you from
so great and ready a Savior?

Jesus' attitude toward his tormentors shows us his readiness to save, and so do his words to this criminal who
looked to him from one cross to the other. In one of his
great doxologies, the apostle Paul says that Jesus does "im-
measurably more than all we ask or imagine" (Eph. 3:20).
That is exactly what we discover in our Lord's reply to this
thief on the cross.

His plea to Christ was quite reserved. He asked that Jesus would remember him, but look what Jesus said: "I tell
you the truth . . . you will be with me in paradise." He asked
only to be remembered, but Jesus says he will be with him.

Furthermore, the thief is looking to the great distant future; his reference to Christ coming into his kingdom
speaks of an end-time deliverance, the kind of which Jesus
so often spoke (see Luke 17:22–37; 22:29–30). But Jesus offers him something far nearer than that. He says, "I tell you
the truth, today you will be with me in paradise."

Imagine, with such words of salvation from the lips of
Christ, the peace with which this man entered into the
arms of death. From a scene straight out of hell, he who was
Jesus' companion on the cross, his last colleague in this life,
entered into a paradise the like of which our eyes have

never beheld, as Christ's first disciple in heaven. Charles Spurgeon writes, "I think the Savior took him with him as a specimen of what he meant to do. He seemed to say to all the heavenly powers, 'I bring a sinner with me; he is a sample of the rest.' "[3]

This scene shows us what Jesus is about with startling clarity. Crucified in utter humiliation, he has only the glory of his saving work. This is his last appearance before the eyes of the world. According to its standards he left in utter defeat. Yet even in the grip of the worst this world could do to him, Jesus goes about his saving business with perfect liberty. When it came to this, nothing in the world could stop him, not even the nails that held him to the cross. What joy this is to the eyes of faith: Jesus leaves this life with a sinner in tow he has just rescued, one more brand plucked from the fire. To the doubting heart, to the guilty conscience, to the burdened soul this gives full assurance of his readiness, his eagerness, and his complete ability to save any and all who come to him in faith. If that is what Jesus could do while nailed to a cross, imagine how able he is to save now that he sits upon the throne of glory and power in heaven.

A Complete Salvation

Jesus is a ready Savior, and he offers to us a complete salvation. This is the fourth and final matter for us to consider. This encounter, culminating in Jesus' statement in Luke 23:43, is a veritable body of divinity on the matter of salvation: "I tell you the truth, today you will be with me in paradise."

First, this thief confirms that salvation is by faith and not by works. He was too late for works but not too late to be saved. If he could be accepted by Christ, on the brink of a lawful execution, then works have no place in the forgiveness of sin. Furthermore, he shows that salvation is instantaneous for those who look to Christ. Jesus emphasized this with his insistence that today this man would be with him. This means that if you will turn to Jesus now, you will be saved now. Immediately upon calling on the Lord your sins are forgiven and you receive the Holy Spirit for newness of life in Christ.

This passage tells us many comforting truths regarding the state of Christians beyond the grave. It tells us that we will be "with the Lord." As Paul says in 2 Corinthians 5:9, while our bodies await the resurrection, our souls are "at home with the Lord." Let me observe in passing how thoroughly this statement from Jesus obliterates the Roman Catholic doctrine of purgatory, where supposedly justified believers yet have the sins Christ died for painfully purged from the soul. This man, though a great sinner up to the hour of his death, did not go to a place of fire but to paradise with our Lord that day.

Then there is this expression Jesus uses, "You will be with me in paradise." To be with Christ in glory is paradise; his presence is what makes heaven a place of such joy. We are meant to recall the paradise garden that was lost by sin in the fall, that afterwards was guarded by the angel with flaming sword. When Jesus says, "You will be with me in paradise," this means his death has opened the way to a better Eden and a more bountiful paradise than our first parents lost. For us the tree of life is none other than the cross of Christ. The cross is the source of our life and the gift of a loving God for those he calls back into fellowship with him forever.

Finally, there is one thing this passage does not teach or encourage, though some foolishly draw the conclusion.

That is the notion that you may safely await the hour of your death to turn to Christ for salvation. The old divines were right, who said, "One was saved upon the cross that none might despair; and only one, that none might presume." Surely the lesson we should draw is the one proclaimed by Paul in 2 Corinthians 6:2, "I tell you, now is the time of God's favor, now is the day of salvation." You do not know the hour or the circumstances of your death, but you do know the consequences of death apart from Christ. Therefore now is the time for you to believe, now is the accepted time for you to be saved.

The Luckiest Man Alive

In one of his devotional books, Philip G. Ryken wrote a chapter on this thief and titled it "The Luckiest Man Alive." This is what he wrote:

> The thief on the cross had to be the luckiest man alive. He was nothing more than a low-life criminal, a loser. He had committed a crime. He was convicted for it, and he was crucified for it. So he had no future; he was going nowhere; or worse, he was going to hell. Yet of all the criminals, on all the crosses, on all the hills in the Roman Empire, he was crucified next to Jesus Christ.[4]

It wasn't impersonal luck that saved the thief but the sovereign mercy of God. But it was fortunate for him. Let me conclude this message by pointing out that it is also fortunate for you when God brings you to a place like his cross. For some it may be a great personal failure, one that makes you face the truth that you are not invincible, you are not so clever as you thought, that you don't have things so safely under control. For others it may be events beyond your control, but they threaten to wipe away your hopes and dreams, your security and peace. For others it may be the day you can no longer bear the burden of your emptiness, can no longer maintain the façade of faked happiness, can no longer deny the aching hole in your life. Realize that when God brings you to that terrible place, to that terrible day, what he means is for you there to open your eyes and, like this thief, to see the Savior he has sent, crucified for you.

If you will look up from that place where God has brought you to gain your attention, if you will look with the eyes of faith, you will find that God has placed you, too, before the Savior Jesus Christ. If you will call out to him the way this thief did from his cross, then that will be your lucky day. Like him, the scene of your despair will become the gateway to paradise. From that day on you will be with Jesus and he will be with you. Because of that, you someday will enter into heaven and even now, this day, heaven will enter into you.

Jesus and the
Downcast Disciples

Luke 24:13–35

They asked each other, "Were not our hearts burning within us while he talked with us on the road and opened the Scriptures to us?" (Luke 24:32)

On the night of his arrest, our Lord Jesus quoted the words of Zechariah 13:7, saying, "It is written: 'I will strike the shepherd, and the sheep of the flock will be scattered'" (Matt. 26:31). That is a sound principle that is repeated over and over in history. The death of Alexander the Great, for instance, produced a dispersion of power in his empire; similarly, when Octavian and Antony killed Brutus and the other leaders of the anti-Caesar faction, the Roman civil war was brought to an end. An excellent biblical example is that of John the Baptist. When Herod put that great prophet to death his followers scattered, just as was true of the many false messiahs history records in the decades after Christ.

It would seem, as we begin this passage, that the same thing was going to happen in the case of Jesus of Nazareth. When last we saw him, our Lord was suffering on the cross and speaking words of salvation to the believing thief. Jesus then died and was buried in a grave. On the third day, his former disciples were scattering in different directions from Jerusalem, the site of their great disappointment and the source of what must have been great fear. This passage in Luke 24 tells the story of two such downcast disciples. By the end of this encounter with Jesus, we will find, however, that here is the exception to the rule Jesus had stated. While Jesus' death initially scattered his flock, it would ultimately serve to bind them together more tightly than ever before. Though initially discouraged, they would become so bold as to turn the world on its head with their gospel. Though dispirited and defeated, Jesus' disciples would, through his death, find their hearts burning with joy and with hope. One fact and one fact only accounts for this marvelous transformation, and that is the fact of his resurrection from the dead.

Jesus the Companion

This passage begins with two disciples, one of whom was named Cleopas, fleeing from Jerusalem to the village of Emmaus. Luke tells us, "They were talking with each other about everything that had happened" (Luke 24:14). We can well imagine how they must have talked after such staggering events, from the triumphal entry to the unjust trials and the culminating crucifixion of Jesus. Surely they were rehashing all of this over and over in their conversation, perhaps trying to imagine how such terrible things could ever have happened. Their general attitude is made clear by the statement of Luke 24:21; theirs was the disappointment of a shattered hope.

Before long, however, footsteps were heard behind them, and then a third traveler caught up with the pair. This newcomer did not hesitate to break into their conversation: "What are you discussing together as you walk along?" he asked.

This is, perhaps, the most instructive of all the postresurrection accounts. Jesus' disciples are heading away from the scene of failure and defeat, leaving a trail of disappointment and despair in their wake. But here we see the risen Lord coming up from behind, his footsteps converging on theirs. Why? Our passage answers that question in three ways. First, he came to encourage his downcast disciples; then, to teach them and correct the ignorance that was causing their despair; and, finally, to reveal himself as the risen, victorious Lord.

Beginning with the first of these, this passage shows beyond a doubt that Jesus Christ delights to walk and talk and be an encouraging companion to his disciples. If that was true on this, the day of his resurrection, then surely it is true of the entire age so powerfully begun.

All of us have had the experience of knowing someone who suddenly is elevated in life. Perhaps it is a roommate or even a close friend, and he or she gets a big promotion, comes into a good deal of money, gets a big break that elevates him or her in status. What is it we usually end up saying? "He's changed." "She's no longer the same person." We are used to people rising up in the world and no longer having time or interest in their old comrades or even looking down their noses on people they used to rub shoulders with.

But none of those examples compare with what had taken place in the case of Jesus. He had died in disgrace, but God raised him from the dead. Paul puts it in the most dramatic terms, that Jesus "through the Spirit of holiness was declared with power to be the Son of God by his resurrection from the dead" (Rom. 1:4). How natural, according to worldly thinking, for him now to think his concern and his dignity far above the realm of his former disciples. One writer, however, observes the opposite:

> Resurrection has not quenched His sympathy. Exalted, He is tender as He was on His humiliation. He is the friendly Lord. He is the companion of His people. His heart yearns with His ancient love. Although bedewed with new glory, He comes close as ever to those His heart approves and pities.[1]

It will be helpful for us to ask what commended these two disciples to Jesus. Was it the excellence of their faith? Was it their importance to his plans? Was it courage and steadfastness that attracted his attention? There is no evidence of any of these. These are disciples we never hear of again; they are not important leaders worthy of Jesus' time for that reason. They were weak believers, at best, fleeing from the shadow of the cross on the resurrection morning. In Luke 24:25 Jesus says to them, "How foolish you are, and how slow of heart to believe all that the prophets have spoken!" They sound like us! These were the kind of disciples Jesus came to walk beside. This shows us, on the first day of the new creation, his deep concern for the lowly and weak among his flock. It proves that fellowship with him depends not on our merit but on his compassion and grace.

Let this comfort you, therefore, that Jesus delights to find you walking, to come up beside you and join you along the way. He walked with his twelve disciples down the paths of Judea. After his resurrection he came along with these two. And now, by his Holy Spirit, he will walk with you if you become his disciple by faith.

Just before his arrest, Jesus was speaking with his disciples in the upper room. He was talking about going away, and they were distressed. Jesus responded to their concerns with the promise of the Holy Spirit. "I will ask the Father," he said, "and he will give you another Counselor to be with you forever— the Spirit of truth. . . . You know him, for he lives with you and will be in you. I will not leave you as orphans; I will come to you. . . . Because I live, you also will live" (John 14:16–19).

Jesus' point was that they would not be without him as they walked the remaining journey of their lives. He would come to them by the Holy Spirit, and in that way he would continue to walk with them, to teach them and reprove them and inspire their hearts. By that same Spirit, Jesus is with us. As the disciples walked with him, we too walk with Jesus. Indeed, this is an acceptable definition of what a Christian is—a Christian is someone who walks with Jesus through faith and by the Holy Spirit.

This does not keep us from the world's troubles, but it makes all the difference in them. When we are afraid, we eagerly speak the words of Psalm 23:4:

> Though I walk
> through the valley of the shadow of death,
> I will fear no evil,
> for you are with me.

One of my favorite passages for comforting the bereaved is
Isaiah 43:2–3, where the Lord says to his people:

> When you pass through the waters,
>   I will be with you;
> and when you pass through the rivers,
>   they will not sweep over you.
> . . . .
> For I am the LORD, your God,
>   the Holy One of Israel, your Savior.

The psalmist rejoiced,

> Blessed are those who have learned to acclaim you,
>   who walk in the light of your presence, O LORD.
>   (Ps. 89:15)

Those are words to describe each and every person who
trusts in Jesus. He will walk with you so that you are never
alone; he will be your companion, all the days of your life.
That is why the writer of Hebrews says:

> Because God has said,
>   "Never will I leave you;
>   never will I forsake you."
> So we say with confidence,
>   "The Lord is my helper; I will not be afraid.
>   What can man do to me?" (Heb. 13:5–6)

Jesus the Teacher

Jesus walks with his own, to comfort them, but he also
speaks with them in order to be their teacher. This course

in Christology on the Emmaus road began with questions, as we have often found in these encounters with Jesus. "What are you discussing together as you walk along?" he began. The two "were kept from recognizing him," we are told without elaboration, and they replied with amazement, "Are you only a visitor to Jerusalem and do not know the things that have happened there in these days?" "What things?" he replied. How often the Holy Spirit speaks with us this way, opening up a dialogue with our hearts and challenging us to reason biblically about our circumstances.

In Luke 24:19–24 we find their answer, which tells us what they had been talking about, as well as their perspective on it. "'About Jesus of Nazareth,' they replied. 'He was a prophet powerful in word and deed before God and all the people.'" This tells us what they understood about Jesus. While this is not a perfect confessional statement, it does show us that they looked upon him as a messianic figure.

Everything they say about Jesus in Luke 24:19 is true and important for us to know. The Greek text begins with an explicit description left out of the New International Version translation: "He was a man." That is a vital truth. He was one of us, though so different as well. They went on, "He was a man, a prophet, mighty in word and deed before God and all the people." A prophet is not merely one who *foretells* the future but mainly *forthtells* the Word of God to the people. This Jesus did with power in word and in deed. Often we are told in the Gospels that the people were amazed when Jesus taught, "because he taught as one who had authority, and not as their teachers of the law" (Matt. 7:29). The same can be said about his many miracles. They revealed the grace and truth and power of God for the salvation of all who look to him in faith. This much these disciples had come to know.

They go on, however, to show how greatly disappointed they were with the events of his crucifixion. "The chief priests and our rulers handed him over to be sentenced to death, and they crucified him; but we had hoped that he was the one who was going to redeem Israel" (Luke 24:20–21). The word *redeem* normally refers to Christ's shed blood as the ransom for the debt of our sin, but it is clear that these disciples were unable to make the connection between his death and that redeeming work, even though they employed the expression.

Furthermore, they had received astounding news that failed to fit within their range of expectation: "In addition," they said, "some of our women amazed us. They went to the tomb early this morning but didn't find his body. They came and told us that they had seen a vision of angels, who said he was alive. Then some of our companions went to the tomb and found it just as the women had said, but him they did not see" (Luke 24:22–24). What a testimony this is to the dullness of the human heart, that people who believed on Jesus and heard these testimonies on the resurrection morning nonetheless headed away in despondent defeat.

Jesus and the Bible

By his questions and their answers, Jesus uncovered the ignorance of these disciples, an ignorance that was the cause of their despondency. How disappointing this attitude was from those who even then were, without knowing it, addressing the risen Lord. This comes through in Jesus' rebuke, "How foolish you are, and how slow of heart to believe all that the prophets have spoken!" They had been shocked by Jesus' apparent ignorance, but now he is shocked by theirs. But Jesus responded to the ignorance of his people not by abandoning or condemning them. His answer is to teach his disciples, and the means by which he does so is the Bible.

This passage is extremely rich in its teaching about the Bible, beginning with *its centrality to the Christian life*. By itself this scene proves the centrality of the Word of God for our instruction in the faith. It would be difficult to overstate the significance that the risen Lord instructs his ignorant followers by means of the Bible. If there were one person we should think would not need the Bible, it would be the resurrected Christ! And yet this is wholly consistent with his attitude elsewhere toward the Scriptures. All through his life, in his private devotion, in his spiritual warfare, and in his public teaching, Jesus had been firmly a man of the Bible, and even after the resurrection we find this unchanged. Surely this says volumes about the attitude all of us should have. Dinsdale Young writes:

> I should have imagined that the Risen Lord would be independent of the Bible. But no! He cleaves to it with all the old affection. He came up from the grave and hastened to the Holy Book. He flooded it with the glory of His countenance, and the precious pages retain the lustre. Nothing reveals to me so clearly the indispensability of the Bible.[2]

What makes the Bible so indispensable is its singular authority as the Word of God. Paul writes in 2 Timothy 3:16 that "all Scripture is God-breathed." We think of the Bible as an *inspired* book, but Paul wants us to think of it as an *expired* revelation, out of the very mouth of God. He adds, therefore, that it "is useful for teaching, rebuking, correcting and training in righteousness, so that the man of God may be thoroughly equipped for every good work."

This means that if you want to grow as a Christian, if you want to learn about God and Jesus, about yourself and the world and salvation as well, then you must commit yourself to the Bible. First, you must receive it as true the way that Jesus did. He said in Matthew 5:18, "I tell you the truth, until heaven and earth disappear, not the smallest letter, not the least stroke of a pen, will by any means disappear from the Law until everything is accomplished." Jesus' view must be yours if you are to profit from the Bible.

Similarly, you must dedicate yourself to its instruction, giving time—preferably each day—to the light of truth that comes from the Bible. The Puritan Thomas Watson writes with characteristic fervor:

> The Word is the field where Christ the pearl of price is hid. In this sacred mine we dig, not for a wedge of gold, but for a weight of glory. . . . The Scripture is the chart and compass by which we sail to the new Jerusalem. . . . Thus, as in the ark manna was laid up, so promises are laid up in the ark of Scripture. The Scripture will make us wise. . . . The Scriptures teach a man to know himself. They discover Satan's snares and stratagems. "They make one wise to salvation" (2 Tim. 3:15). Oh, then, highly prize the Scriptures.[3]

That is the first thing we see about the Bible, its centrality to the Christian life as the authoritative and powerful Word of God. The second lesson is *the Bible's subject matter*. Jesus said, and this is a significant passage for Bible interpretation, " 'Did not the Christ have to suffer these things and then enter his glory?" And beginning with Moses and all the Prophets, he explained to them what was said in all the Scriptures concerning himself" (Luke 24:26–27). The Bible speaks to many topics, indeed to all of life, and yet *its principal subject is the person and work of Jesus Christ.*

This is why Jesus saw fit to reprove the two disciples, because the need for the Redeemer to suffer and die is plainly spoken of in the Old Testament, and remember, it is the Old Testament he has in view. Where, we ask, is Jesus found in the Old Testament? Is it just in select passages— say, Isaiah 53 or Psalm 22? No, it is in "all the Scriptures" that Jesus is to be found.

Imagine being in these disciples' shoes. "Beginning with Moses," Jesus taught them—that means Genesis 1, which begins, "In the beginning God created the heavens and the earth. . . . And God said, 'Let there be light,' and there was light" (Gen. 1:1–3). Surely Jesus explained with words like those we find in John 1:1–2, "In the beginning was the Word, and the Word was with God, and the Word was God. He was with God in the beginning." That is talking about him, Jesus, the incarnate Word. On he went through the whole Old Testament, through Moses and then the prophets, "he explained to them what was said in all the Scriptures concerning himself." That means that the answer to the Old Testament, the key to the whole Bible, is Jesus Christ. If we read the Old Testament without seeing him, then we are not reading it rightly. The evangelist Harry Ironside wrote:

> Our Lord Jesus Christ is the Spirit of the Old Testament. Turn where you will in the Old Testament, it has one theme, and that is Christ. He is the Spirit

of the whole thing, and if you just see the letter but do not see Him, you have missed the purpose for which God gave His Book.[4]

It is not that everything to be known about Jesus is found in every Old Testament passage, nor even is that true in the New Testament. But, as John Owen explains:

> God has distributed the light of Christ's glory through the whole firmament of the Scriptures. Each part gives off its own light for the building up of the church's faith. One part of Scripture describes his person and glory clearly and plainly, whereas other parts present it in allegories conveying a heavenly sense of them to the minds of believers. Yet other parts describe his glory in his exaltation and his power. As one star differs from another in glory, so God revealed the glory of Christ under the Old Testament types and shadows, and more fully under the New Testament. Glorious testimonies to these things are planted in all parts of Scripture which we might gather as Eve might have gathered flowers in the paradise of God.[5]

Jesus the Revealer

Our passage concludes with a description of what it means to encounter Jesus, as these two disciples did on that road, as all the subjects of our study of encounters with Jesus did, and as we encounter him in the pages of his Holy Word. We have seen him in this passage as Jesus the companion, as Jesus the teacher, and here we see him as Jesus the revealer.

These disciples drew near to their destination, and they urged Jesus to join them. "Stay with us," they said, "for it is nearly evening; the day is almost over" (Luke 24:29). Jesus therefore went in with them. There at the table "he took bread, gave thanks, broke it and began to give it to them" (v. 30). Surely we are intended by these words to think of the Last Supper and to realize it is to be the ongoing experience of his people to have that fellowship with him. It was then that this meal was revealed as a true communion service. "Their eyes were opened and they recognized him, and he disappeared from their sight. They asked each other, 'Were not our hearts burning within us while he talked with us on the road and opened the Scriptures to us?' " (vv. 31–32).

I said at the beginning that it is the resurrection that explains the courage and passion of these followers of a leader who had died. The reason is that the fruit of his resurrection is the new birth, and the new birth is what empowered the bold and courageous faith of these early disciples. Jesus rose from the dead and sent a new principle of life into the hearts of his people.

The main effect of this rebirth is that Jesus is revealed to their once-blind eyes. That is what it means to be born again, to see Jesus as Lord and Savior with the eyes of faith. That is also the primary work of God's Holy Spirit, as Jesus said in John 15:26, "When the Counselor comes, whom I will send to you from the Father, the Spirit of truth who goes out from the Father, he will testify about me." This is the goal of his encounters with us. "Now this is eternal life," he had prayed in John 17:3, "that they may know you, the only true God, and Jesus Christ, whom you have sent." This is the true goal for which Jesus came up behind these two on the road; it is the goal for which he walks with us in this life, that we would know him and God through him. This should be the object of our Bible study, to find him and to learn of him, yes, but more—to know him and see him as he is spiritually revealed to our Spirit-quickened hearts.

I find it fascinating that these two realized they were sitting down to meal with Jesus, and yet it is of the Word that they spoke. What they marveled at was not just seeing Jesus risen from the dead but also understanding the biblical revelation about him. This is why Peter wrote, "For you have been born again, not of perishable seed, but of imperishable, through the living and enduring word of God" (1 Peter 1:23). That is what made them exclaim with joy: "Were not our hearts burning within us?"

That is what happens if you encounter Jesus: The scales fall from your eyes as he shines his light on the Word, igniting there a fire for him in your heart. As once the fire burned with the bush in the presence of Moses, so when we encounter Jesus in his Word that same fire burns in us. It is the work of his Holy Spirit, and it is the object of all his work, that God should dwell within us and that like these two disciples we should draw near to him. This is what we find in Luke 24:33, "They got up and returned at once to Jerusalem." There they found the Eleven, and they joined into that first Easter throng, the redeemed at the dawn of the new creation in Christ.

Encounters with Jesus

As we look back over the various encounters with Jesus we have examined in this book, we find that these two once downcast and now enflamed disciples illustrate what it means to come face to face with him. To encounter Jesus is to encounter the Lord, to be called to receive him by faith and be changed forever. Those who have encountered

Jesus in faith inevitably exclaim, "Were not our hearts burning within us?"

We think back to Nicodemus and how he was presented with the need for a complete change of paradigm. Two things, Jesus told him, must take place: Nicodemus must be born again and Jesus must be lifted on the cross (John 3:7, 14). We look in Luke 24:26, and Jesus says the same to these two disciples: "Did not the Christ have to suffer these things and then enter his glory?" Yes, he did. He suffered to redeem us from our sin by his blood, and he was raised to life to secure for us the new birth we see manifested in their hearts. Nicodemus left Jesus with only a spark smoldering in his breast, but by the end of John's Gospel it had ignited into the same kind of flame these two disciples experienced.

The same might be said of the woman by the well in John 4. She found in him one who not only gave her answers but also was the Answer. As she spread the word to her neighbors, she must have said, "My heart is burning within me!" Imagine what must have gone through the adulterous woman's mind, when Jesus first chased off her accusers, then turned to her, saying, "Neither do I condemn you. Go now and leave your life of sin" (John 8:11). Isn't this what Zacchaeus would have said if asked what made him repent of a lifetime spent in greed and selfishness? "My heart is burning for Jesus!" And surely it was with that same burning heart that the condemned thief departed from this world into paradise with Jesus.

John the Baptist said, in the days before Jesus' ministry began: "I baptize you with water. But one more powerful than I will come, the thongs of whose sandals I am not worthy to untie. He will baptize you with the Holy Spirit and with fire" (Luke 3:16). That is what an encounter with Jesus is all about. This is not talking about some fleshly experience; that is not the burning in the heart that is from God. "The kingdom of God is not a matter of eating and drinking," Paul wrote, "but of righteousness, peace and joy in the Holy Spirit" (Rom. 14:17). That is the dwelling of God within our hearts, like the burning bush of old.

If you will seek Jesus in his Word, as it is preached and as you read it in the Bible, and if you will believe on him who suffered for you and then went ahead into glory, that same Spirit will come to reveal him to your heart, igniting there a fire that will never go out because it is of God. That is what every encounter with Jesus is about, that you would receive him through faith and enter into life everlasting, beginning now with new life within, a light for your mind and a fire to warm your heart. Then you too will hasten back to be with him, you will turn back down the road toward Jerusalem, and you will join that resurrection community in the light of the open tomb.

Notes

chapter 1: Jesus and the Scholar

1 Leon Morris, *The Gospel According to John* (Grand Rapids, Mich.: Eerdmans, 1995), 188.
2 J. C. Ryle, *Expository Thoughts on the Gospels*, John, 2 vols. (London: James Clark, 1975), 1:122.
3 "Water and spirit" are linked rather than contrasted. They together fill the space occupied by "from above" in John 3:3 and therefore do not likely point to two different births, one of which is not "from above." A lucid discussion of these matters is found in D. A. Carson, *The Gospel According to John* (Grand Rapids, Mich.: Eerdmans, 1991), 191–97.
4 D. Martyn Lloyd-Jones, *Safe in the World* (Wheaton, Ill.: Crossway, 1988), 91.
5 See "Jennings on Jesus," *Christianity Today*, June 12, 2000, 72–73.
6 Morris, *Gospel According to John*, 189.
7 G. Campbell Morgan, *The Gospel According to John* (Westwood, N.J.: Revell, n.d.), 60.

chapter 2: Jesus and the Woman at the Well

1 Cf. Leon Morris, *The Gospel According to John* (Grand Rapids, Mich.: Eerdmans, 1995), 228.

2 Arthur W. Pink, *The Seven Sayings of the Saviour on the Cross* (Grand Rapids, Mich.: Baker, 1958), 96.
3 Augustine, *The Confessions* (Oxford: Oxford University Press, 1991), 3.
4 "Come to the Waters," from James Montgomery Boice and Paul S. Jones, *Hymns for a Modern Reformation* (Philadelphia: Tenth Music, 2000), 20.
5 John Calvin, *The Gospel According to St. John*, 2 vols. (Grand Rapids, Mich.: Eerdmans, 1989), 1:104.

chapter 3: Jesus and the Man by the Pool

1 Patrick O'Brian, *Desolation Island* (New York: Norton, 1978), 146.
2 See D. A. Carson, *The Gospel According to John* (Grand Rapids, Mich.: Eerdmans, 1991), 241–42.
3 James Montgomery Boice, *The Gospel of John* (Grand Rapids, Mich.: Zondervan, 1985), 307.
4 John Calvin, *Sermons on Ephesians* (Carlisle, Pa.: Banner of Truth, 1973), 37.
5 William Barclay, *The Gospel of John*, rev. ed., 2 vols. (Philadelphia: Westminster, 1975), 1:180.
6 Arthur W. Pink, *Exposition of the Gospel of John*, 2 vols. (Grand Rapids, Mich.: Zondervan, 1945), 1:253.

chapter 4: Jesus and the Woman Caught in Adultery

1 J. Duncan M. Derrett, *New Testament Studies* 10 (1963–64): 4–5.
2 Arthur W. Pink, *Exposition of the Gospel of John*, 2 vols. (Grand Rapids, Mich.: Zondervan, 1945), 2:11–12.
3 John Calvin, *The Gospel According to St. John*, 2 vols. (Grand Rapids, Mich.: Eerdmans, 1989), 1:206.
4 Pink, *Exposition of the Gospel of John*, 2:13.
5 James Montgomery Boice, *The Gospel of John* (Grand Rapids, Mich.: Zondervan, 1985), 516.
6 Calvin, *The Gospel According to St. John*, 1:208.
7 Martin Luther, *Luther's Works*, ed. Jaroslav Pelikan, 55 vols., *Sermons on the Gospel of John, Ch. 6–8* (St. Louis: Concordia, 1959), 23:318–19.

chapter 5: Jesus and the Fisherman

1 Dietrich Bonhoeffer: *The Cost of Discipleship* (New York: Collier, 1937), 47.
2 Ibid., 99.
3 Ibid.
4 Charles Haddon Spurgeon, *The Parables and Miracles of Our Lord*, 3 vols. (Grand Rapids, Mich.: Baker, 1993), 2:462–63.
5 Roland H. Bainton, *Here I Stand* (Penguin: New York, 1955), 30.
6 R. C. Sproul, *The Holiness of God* (Wheaton, Ill.: Tyndale, 1985), 126.
7 Ibid., 44.
8 Martin Luther, *Sermons of Martin Luther: The Church Postils*, 8 vols. (Grand Rapids, Mich.: Baker, 1995), 4:156.
9 Bonhoeffer, *The Cost of Discipleship*, 99.

chapter 6: Jesus and the Tax Collector

1 John Calvin, *A Harmony of the Gospels*, 3 vols. (Grand Rapids, Mich.: Eerdmans, 1971), 1:262.
2 Charles Haddon Spurgeon, "A Man Named Matthew," in *Metropolitan Tabernacle Pulpit*, 63 vols. (Carlisle, Pa.: Banner of Truth, 1971), 42:773.
3 Augustine, *On the Spirit and the Letter*, from *The Nicene and Post-Nicene Fathers*, vol. 5, *Saint Augustine: Anti-Pelagian Writings* (Edinburgh: T & T Clark, 1991), 106.

chapter 7: Jesus and the Sinful Woman

1 Harry A. Ironside, *Addresses on the Gospel of Luke* (Neptune, N.J.: Loizeaux Brothers, 1988), 230.
2 Donald Grey Barnhouse: *Exposition of Bible Doctrines Taking the Epistle to the Romans as a Point of Departure*, 10 vols. (Grand Rapids, Mich.: Eerdmans, 1953), 2:81.
3 Alexander Maclaren: *Sermons for All Seasons* (Grand Rapids, Mich.: World, 1995), 26.
4 John Owen: *The Glory of Christ* (Carlisle, Pa.: Banner of Truth, 1994), 117.

5 Arthur W. Pink, *Comfort for Christians* (Grand Rapids, Mich.: Baker, 1976), 14, 15.

6 Charles Haddon Spurgeon, "Love's Competition," in *The Metropolitan Tabernacle Pulpit*, 63 vols. (Carlisle, Pa.: Banner of Truth, 1973), 36:81.

7 Charles Haddon Spurgeon, "A Visit to Calvary," *Spurgeon's Sermons*, 10 vols. (Grand Rapids, Mich.: Baker, n.d), 2:339.

8 J. I. Packer: *Knowing God* (Downers Grove, Ill.: InterVarsity Press, 1973), 114.

chapter 8: Jesus and the Little Children

1 William Barclay, *The Gospel of Matthew*, 2 vols. (Philadelphia: Westminster, 1958), 2:233.

2 Ibid., 2:234.

3 J. C. Ryle, *Expository Thoughts on Mark* (Carlisle, Pa.: Banner of Truth, 1985), 202.

4 Ibid., 202–3.

5 James Montgomery Boice, "Children's Sermons," *Modern Reformation*, November/December 1999, 52.

6 R. C. Sproul, *A Walk with Jesus* (Ross-shire, UK: Christian Focus, 1999), 293–94.

chapter 9: Jesus and the Rich Young Man

1 Alexander Maclaren, *Expositions of Holy Scripture*, 11 vols. (Grand Rapids, Mich.: Eerdmans, 1959), 5:76–77.

2 Charles Haddon Spurgeon, "Lovely but Lacking," *Metropolitan Tabernacle Pulpit*, 63 vols. (Carlisle, Pa.: Banner of Truth, 1973), 58:775.

3 J. C. Ryle, *Expository Thoughts on Mark* (Carlisle, Pa.: Banner of Truth, 1985), 212.

chapter 10: Jesus and the Man in the Tree

1 C. S. Lewis, *Surprised by Joy* (New York: HarperCollins, 1985), 124.

2 Ibid., 125.

3 Alfred Edersheim, *The Life and Times of Jesus the Messiah* (Peabody, Mass.: Hendrickson, n.d.), 352.

4 Matthew Henry, *Commentary on the Whole Bible*, 6 vols. (Peabody, Mass.: Hendrickson, 1992), 5:631.

5 J. C. Ryle, *Expository Thoughts on the Gospels*, Luke, 2 vols. (Carlisle, Pa.: Banner of Truth, 1976), 2:295.

chapter 11: Jesus and the Governor

1 Augustine, *City of God* (New York: Doubleday, 1950), 14.28.

2 James Montgomery Boice, *The Gospel of John* (Grand Rapids, Mich.: Zondervan, 1985), 1278.

3 D. Martyn Lloyd-Jones, *The Cross* (Westchester, Ill.: Crossway, 1986), 99.

chapter 12: Jesus and the Thief on the Cross

1 Donald Grey Barnhouse, *Exposition of Bible Doctrines Taking the Epistle to the Romans as a Point of Departure*, 10 vols. (Grand Rapids, Mich.: Eerdmans, 1953), 2:161.

2 Alexander Maclaren, *Expositions of Holy Scripture*, 11 vols. (Grand Rapids, Mich.: Eerdmans, 1959), 6:312–13.

3 Charles Haddon Spurgeon, "The Believing Thief," in *The Metropolitan Tabernacle Pulpit*, 63 vols. (Carlisle, Pa.: Banner of Truth, 1973), 35:241.

4 Philip Graham Ryken, with James Montgomery Boice, *The Heart of the Cross* (Wheaton, Ill.: Crossway, 1999), 21.

chapter 13: Jesus and the Downcast Disciples

1 Dinsdale T. Young, "Three Phases of the Risen Christ," in Wilber M. Smith, *Great Sermons on the Resurrection of Christ* (Natick, Mass.: W. A. Wilde, 1964), 88.

2 Ibid., 90.

3 Thomas Watson: *A Body of Divinity* (Carlisle, Pa.: Banner of Truth, 1958), 36.

4 Harry A. Ironside, *Second Corinthians* (Neptune, N.J.: Loizeaux Brothers, 1939), 91.

5 John Owen: *The Glory of Christ* (Carlisle, Pa.: Banner of Truth, 1994), 122–23.

Discussion Questions

chapter 1: Jesus and the Scholar

1. Describe the setting in which Jesus encounters Nicodemus (John 3:1–21).

2. What type of man does Nicodemus represent? What sorts of things could make it hard for a man like Nicodemus to have faith in Jesus? What about you and others you know?

3. In verse 3, what does Jesus reveal to Nicodemus? Nicodemus claims to know many things. What is the right way to pursue knowledge of God?

4. What are some common but false views about the rebirth?

5. Explain the three points Jesus teaches about the rebirth. Can you find support for them elsewhere in Scripture?

6. How can we know we are born again? What visible effects of the rebirth can you see in your own life?

7. What is the relationship between the rebirth and the cross? How is the rebirth a product of God's love for us?

Chapter 13: Jesus and the Downcast Disciples

1. The encounter with the two men on the Emmaus road presents Jesus as a companion walking beside his disciples (Luke 24:13–35). What does it mean to walk with God? Do you experience this and how? What did Jesus say in John 14:16–19 about his gift of the Holy Spirit?

2. Why are the disciples downcast? What causes Christians today to be discouraged and defeated? How do you deal with this?

3. The downcast disciples describe Jesus as "a man, a prophet, mighty in word and deed." How is this an accurate description of Jesus? What does it leave out?

4. What does this encounter tell us about Jesus' view of the Bible? How should we think of the Bible? How do you give priority to God's Word in your own life?

5. The author states that the Bible's "principal subject is the person and work of Jesus Christ." How is Jesus present all through the Bible, especially in the Old Testament? What does this tell us about what we should be looking for in the Bible?

6. The author describes Jesus' meal with the disciples as "a true communion service." Do you partake of the Lord's Supper in a church? How is this a spiritual blessing to you?

7. When the disciples realize that Jesus has risen and met with them, how do they respond? How are their lives different as a result?

8. When people encounter Jesus, their hearts burn within them. Have you experienced this? If not, why not? If so, how should you respond to the precious gift of God's wonderful saving grace?

Index of Scripture

Richard D. Phillips (B.A., University of Michigan; M.B.A., University of Pennsylvania; M.Div., Westminster Theological Seminary) is minister of preaching at historic Tenth Presbyterian Church in Philadelphia. He is also speaker-at-large for the Alliance of Confessing Evangelicals and host of *The Bible Study Hour* radio program. He leads the Reformation Societies, a grass roots endeavor to mobilize Christian leaders across the nation in support of biblical reformation.

An officer in the United States Army for thirteen years, Phillips commanded various tank and armored cavalry units and served as assistant professor of leadership at the United States Military Academy, West Point, before resigning with the rank of major.

He is the author of *Mighty to Save: Discovering God's Grace in the Miracles of Jesus* and *The Heart of an Executive: Lessons on Leadership from the Life of King David*. He lives in Philadelphia with his wife, Sharon, and their three children, Hannah, Matthew, and Jonathan.